A

# Beating
# Depression

Published under licence by Brown Dog Books and The Self-Publishing Partnership, 7 Green Park Station, Bath BA1 1JB

www.selfpublishingpartnership.co.uk

ISBN printed book: 978-1-83952-111-9
ISBN e-book: 978-1-83952-112-6

Cover design by Kevin Rylands
Internal design by Andrew Easton

Printed and bound by CPI Group (UK) Ltd, Croydon CR0 4YY

This book is printed on FSC certified paper

# A Practical Guide to Beating Depression

Written by **Charlie Wardle**

# Table of Contents

# A quick introduction...

Wouldn't it be nice if there was a magic wand or a magic pill that could instantly make you feel happier and not be depressed? Unfortunately there isn't, but then again if there was then that wouldn't be as interesting or rewarding as understanding, and then beating, depression for yourself!

Many people will experience depression in its various forms, and for many reasons, yet most will never really understand why. They won't know why they feel, think, and behave the way they do, or what are the reasons and triggers for depression. But you can! Moreover, with the knowledge and understanding and the control that brings, you can beat depression forever.

I strongly believe that everybody can beat depression if they have the understanding and the tools and techniques necessary to manage and prevent it – but that isn't easy and sometimes you need a helping hand, and I am here to give you that hand. However, before I do, let's go back to what I need from you throughout this book:

**Effort** – You get out what you put in. So live, breathe and embrace this book over the next few weeks – you will see the rewards.

**Patience** – As the saying goes, a little patience goes a long way.

You may start feeling improvements from day one; you may not realise them until the end. However, either way, if you have the patience and perseverance, you will get there.

**Practice** – Practice makes perfect and it is key to beating depression. Practice the techniques throughout the book in order to reinforce the thoughts, beliefs, and actions. The more you practice, the easier it becomes and the greater the results.

**Desire** – I already know you want this because you have read this far. If you have the desire, you will get the results. So never forget why you turned to this book in the first place. You can beat depression, and think how much better your life will be in the future.

I know you won't need it, but good luck! If you get stuck, have questions, want to provide feedback, or just want to let me know how you are getting on, contact me via the website www.climbyourmountain.org.

I wish you the very best. Now go for it!
**Charlie Wardle**
Founder of Climb Your Mountain (CYM)
www.climbyourmountain.org

# How to Use This Book

This book is split into eight chapters and it is important to ensure you read through and understand each chapter to get the full benefits and therefore give you the best opportunity to beat depression for good.

I know that depression can be very difficult to deal with, and the thought of beating it is an exciting prospect, but rushing through the book quickly may mean that you don't gain the full benefit of the information, exercises, and time to think and reflect.

I also know that life is busy and can get in the way, but dedicating a few hours per week to reading the content, and a few minutes a day to practising the exercises, means that you will have every chance to beat depression and significantly improve your life as a result.

The book has lots of questions, exercises, and reflection time as well as information. Make sure you complete all of these and give the exercises your all. Be honest with yourself and your answers – if this means that you would rather not write something down, that is fine as long as you are truthful with yourself. Take your time to really think about any questions posed and your answers and, although it is very much about your own thoughts, it may be useful to ask a close friend, partner, or family member their thoughts, so that you can gain a different perspective. You never know, their answers might surprise you.

Spread your commitment to this book however best works for you, but commit yourself to making that time, and make that commitment now. You already know this, but it will be reiterated throughout the book, that the more you put in, then the more you get out. The effort will be rewarded and the more you learn, understand, apply, and practise, then the more your confidence will grow in beating depression once and for all.

Each chapter starts with the objectives, and before you proceed to the following chapter make sure that you feel you have fulfilled those objectives. If you cannot do this it may be that you need to complete the exercises or that you need more time to absorb the information presented. Don't worry if this is you; some chapters will be harder than others.

If you do get stuck please feel free to contact me via the website www.climbyourmountain.org or proceed to the next chapter but make a note to return to that pending objective later on.

# Introduction

Many people will experience depression. There are many different types of depression and many reasons why it manifests itself. There are many people who do not realise they have depression, and some people who think they have depression but in fact they do not. Depression can be the cause of many other issues and it can also be the result or effect of many other issues. There is no doubt that it is complicated, and most people have very little knowledge or understanding of what it is, why it happens, and what they can do to overcome it.

However, my belief is that in most cases it can be understood and can be overcome. It will take effort and time, and the most effective way to ensure the best results is to understand it yourself and work out why it happens and what you can do about it for you. You can beat depression!

I say this based upon several years of research, reading about it, talking to people, thinking about it, understanding it the best I can, PLUS I have had my own experiences of depression. As I have already said, there are many types of depression, varying degrees of severity, and many particular reasons and factors involved as to why it occurs. However, I am happy to share my particular story and I hope that, like myself, you can understand, gain the knowledge, develop the tools, and then beat depression so it no longer has to play any part in your life again going forward.

# My story

October 2003 was my lowest point, where I felt so empty, numb, and alone. I couldn't believe what was happening and how I was feeling. My life wasn't supposed to be like this, and if this was my life, then what was the point? I had put so much effort in, worked so hard, done everything I could and yet I was in this position. It wasn't right, it wasn't fair, and I didn't understand it.

It would be over five years later that I really started to understand what had really happened to me, why I reacted the way I did, why I felt the way I did, and the fact that at that time, and for the next few years, I was experiencing a type of depression. I was a successful person in lots of ways. I was intelligent, well educated, a qualified accountant with one of the most prestigious firms in the world, and in 2002 had completed an MBA from one of the world's leading business schools. I had many other qualifications, I had been in senior positions at large companies, had owned houses, had run marathons, been very sporty, and been told I wasn't bad-looking! I was 29 years of age.

I also knew nothing about depression.

I was ambitious and always believed I would be successful and wealthy. My family never had much money and it was often an issue growing up, so becoming wealthy was always a goal probably as a response to that. I had done well with my career to date and after completing the MBA in 2002 I set up a business in the sports industry. All was going well and it had real potential, but without going into all the detail we needed more capital and the route suggested was a business loan with a bank, but secured personally so that we had access straight away. I never saw it as a problem until things started to go wrong.

We were working long hours, putting in a huge amount of effort, yet it seemed that increasingly other people and companies we were working with were letting us down: not delivering what they say they would, being unreliable and, in many cases, completely useless. I had put all the money I had into the business and now had to take out a loan to cover living costs, and the financial position of the business worsened.

It felt as if no matter how much effort I put in, other people would cause issues that would cost us money. My personal debt kept growing, with the combination of the business loan and personal loan, and at the same time these other people were responsible, or at least it felt like that. Day after day, I would do everything I could, more and more effort to make things work, but the same things kept happening with people not delivering as they should, yet we were paying the cost. And not just financially.

In October, I took the decision to end the business. I said it was because my personal debt, with interest, was now about £100k and I had to do something else to earn some money. The financial side was a major factor but the reality was I had nothing else to give. I was empty. Everything seemed so wrong and unfair. How could this have happened?

I had no more drive left in me. For someone who was always a 'go-getter' and very proactive it was a very strange feeling and I didn't know what to do. I stayed in bed for two days, just numb. I was 29 years of age with about £100k of debt, yet I had worked so hard and put so much effort in. Other people had not done what they should have done and I had paid the price. How was that right? I was always led to believe that you get out what you put in, and if you work hard and do the right things then you will be successful.

I felt I had failed. I was empty and numb. I was alone and I really didn't see what the point was anymore.

Anyway, after a couple of days I forced myself to get out of bed and I took stock of the situation. All I could think about was the money and the debt. I had to get a job and start paying it back as soon as possible. I had a good CV and was fortunate to secure a decent job very quickly. However, it was back working in finance as an accountant and I really didn't enjoy that or want to be doing it, but it was my best way of earning decent money. Again, without going into all the detail, I worked really hard over the next few years to pay back all the debt. It took me just under three and a half years.

During this time, it felt like I was leading a double life. People who knew me at work saw me as a successful high-flier, earning lots of money in senior positions. I was pretty fit and healthy, and had retained my youthful good looks. No doubt some people were envious, as it did look like I was doing very well for myself as I entered my early thirties.

The reality was very different. I didn't realise it, but I was depressed. I knew nothing about depression at that point. All I knew was that I was sad, unhappy and miserable, and had become a virtual recluse. I didn't really feel like going out and being sociable, but the main reason was that it cost money and literally every penny I had was scrutinised so that as much as possible would go to paying back the debt. I couldn't afford luxuries like going out, meeting friends, and enjoying life.

During this period I cried a lot, feeling sorry for myself, and my only reason for living seemed to be this challenge of paying back the debt so that I could restart my life. Each time I cried I would get angry with myself. How could I be crying? I was a strong person, a natural leader, a go-getter, a fighter, so how on earth was this happening? It made no sense and I didn't feel in control of my emotions. It sometimes took every ounce of what I had left in me not to cry at work. I was in a senior position for a very large, well-known company, often meeting with directors. What on earth would they think if I started crying?

Anyway, the day came in early summer 2007 when I finally paid off all the debt. I was no longer a prisoner and I could start my life again. I had spent so long waiting for this moment, having put my life on hold for so long doing nothing but working hard, paying off the debt, and being depressed. Well, it was a huge anticlimax and the reality was that I was back to zero. It was as if, rather than having climbed a mountain, all I had done was climb out of a deep pit and now I was at the bottom of the mountain with that still to climb.

I then wrote a book about my experiences. It was about 80,000 words and I called it *The Joy of Debt* (not published!). It was a very personal account but the process was very cathartic and it was really helpful to put so much onto paper that was whirling around in my head. One of the things in the book that stood out to me was the fact that during those three and a half years I had run the Las Vegas and the Toronto Marathons.

At the time of doing these marathons, I didn't really think much of it. Rightly or wrongly, it was a way for me to get a free holiday as I was able to raise lots of money from work and do it for charity, so it was good for the charity and good for me. I did a bit of training and then completed a marathon in a fantastic location. Looking back, I realised that actually it was really beneficial for me and positive in an otherwise very negative and depressing period of my life. It made me think about how beneficial physical exercise and challenges could be to people who might be going through a tough time for whatever reason.

I also started thinking about what I would like to do with my life if money didn't matter. My answer was to set something up that would help anyone going through a difficult time, like I had, and encourage them to do a physical challenge. If someone had their own personal mountain to climb, then I wanted to help them climb that mountain.

However, I had no money and I had promised myself I would never have any debt again and so I needed to continue with my finance career, earn lots of money, save lots of money, and then I could consider doing something else. So I became a finance director of a large global company. My plan was to do this for a few years and then set up a charity called Climb Your Mountain, to encourage people to do physical activities and challenges to help them through a difficult time in their life.

I left my finance career behind and set up the charity in April 2008. It was a huge, life-defining decision in so many ways!

I had no previous experience of the charity sector or what would be involved and, although I had initial enthusiasm and there were things I could get on with, like setting up a website and producing and delivering flyers, there were also many brick walls I hit straight away. Setting up a registered charity is not straightforward, and I encountered months of difficulties, frustrations, and let-downs. Finding any kind of support or funding was just as troublesome. Furthermore, it seemed that everyone I was dealing with in terms of setting up, supporting, or funding the charity didn't really care and nothing seemed to get done quickly.

I was constantly banging my head against a brick wall and I couldn't understand what was happening again. I had given up a very well-paid job to set up something to help people with my own money and do something good, yet I was feeling worse and worse. I carried on and kept putting in the effort, but although it became an official registered charity in September 2008, I was not in a good place. Many of the symptoms I had experienced a few years before were coming back and, although I didn't realise it, I was suffering with depression again.

It was in November 2008, whilst driving home one evening from a meeting, that I heard that a book by the cricketer Marcus Trescothick had won the Sports Book of Year award. It was not only about his career, but also about the depression he had which ultimately ended his international career. A few days later I had bought a copy and started to read it. Over the next few days I read it cover to cover and several things resonated with me. A few things started to make more sense and I was intrigued enough to straight away buy a book he recommended subtitled *The Curse of the Strong*, which I mention later. I read this book straight away and so much more made sense. Over the next couple of months, I read several more books and did a lot of research.

I was suffering with depression and it all made sense! I was now aware that it was a stress-related form of depression, which I had previously had, and I was much more susceptible to it due to my personality and character. I was both sad at the fact that this is what I was going through, and what I had previously gone through, yet there was a relief that after such a long time it now all made sense and I started to feel more in control.

I kept reading and researching over the coming months and then decided to start delivering courses on what I now knew. I realised that education and knowledge were key to anyone wanting to climb their own mountain. You need to understand, to make sense, to feel in control, to have the knowledge, and to know why and what to do that will help. Over the next few years, I delivered hundreds of courses and workshops to thousands of people on a wide range of health and wellbeing subjects, including depression.

Personally, I now feel 100% confident that I will never suffer with depression again due to the knowledge and understanding I now have and the tools and techniques I have developed to prevent and manage depression effectively. Once you have the knowledge and the tools, then you can control the depression rather than the depression controlling you.

# Chapter 1

# Small Steps First

*Objectives:*
*This chapter is all about starting with the small things that will make a*
*big difference in beating depression. Particularly focused on everyday*
*thinking and behaviours, and what you can do to help make some*
*positive changes. The earlier you start doing this, the easier it becomes*
*and the more effective.*

## Turning the ship around

A good analogy to use is to think of yourself as a big cruise ship on the ocean and right now you are heading in the wrong direction, or at least you think you are. You may feel lost, with no idea where you are heading, but you know it doesn't feel right; you don't feel in control and you don't know what you can do about it. Many people feel like this and you are certainly not alone, even if at times you think it is just you.

What you need to do, using this analogy, is to try to work out where you are and where you need to be going, and then to turn your big cruise ship around onto the right setting. None of that is easy and it will not be quick; however, it is achievable. You will work out where you are and where you need to go (and why you went off course) and then you can be in control and turn the ship around.

With a cruise ship you cannot simply turn it around so it will take time to change direction, so imagine yourself on that ocean slowly but surely turning the ship around as you gain the knowledge and understanding as to where you need to go.

| Describe your general feelings, thoughts, and behaviours | How would you like to feel, think, and behave |
|---|---|
| e.g. tired, unmotivated, empty | Have more energy, look forward to things, drink less |

## Positive & Productive

If you look at the table above I am sure that most, if not all, of the feelings, thoughts, and behaviours you have listed on the left side are negative and unproductive. In contrast, on the right-hand side they are no doubt much more positive and productive. Of course, you would much rather your life be full of the positive and productive things and be living on that right-hand side.

No matter what you may currently be thinking and feeling, this is possible and will be the case in the future, if you see this book through. One of the most positive and productive things you can start doing right now is recognising the difference between the two sides – positive and productive vs. negative and unproductive. Each day think carefully about what you are doing, thinking, saying, behaving like, and recognise how much of it is positive and how much is negative. It may help to write these down as and when you recognise them. Get two pieces of paper –one for all the negative stuff and one for the positive stuff.

You know that the negative and unproductive stuff is not helping you and won't help beat depression. So do your best to stop these thoughts and feelings as soon as you recognise them. It will be difficult, especially at first, but once you start making a real conscious effort it will become easier – I guarantee it. And whenever you have any positive thoughts or do something productive then make a note, write it down, think about it, hang onto it, and praise yourself. This is hard to do at the moment so make sure you recognise it and give yourself a pat on the back. For some people it is no big deal and feels completely normal, but for you right now that is not the case, so make a deal of it and make sure you recognise those positive and productive actions.

Fill in the table below, thinking about your own thoughts and behaviours:

| Examples of negative and and unproductive thoughts and and behaviours | Examples of positive productive thoughts behaviours |
|---|---|
| e.g. thinking nothing ever goes right for me, and I am so unlucky | e.g. thinking that there are so many potentially good things to look forward to and I want to do my best to make those happen |
| e.g. I don't feel like going outside, so I will just shut myself away at home | e.g. it's a nice day and I'm going to take a walk around the park to get some fresh air and reflect on a few things |
| | |

## Stopping the spiral of decline and creating your toolbox

Many people do, and will, suffer with some type of depression. If the statistics are right, then one in five people will be directly affected by depression, and therefore it stands to reason that pretty much everyone will be affected indirectly by knowing somebody who is suffering.

There are many types of depression and many factors that can cause it. Stress-related depression is one of the main types and is becoming more recognised. Alongside this, one of the most common aggravating factors is negative thinking. Negative thinking causes more negative thinking and thinking in a negative way compounds the depression. It becomes a vicious circle whereby the more depressed you are, the more negative thinking results, and the more negative thinking, the more depressed you become.

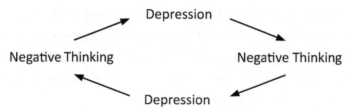

Of course, the answer is to stop thinking negatively. However, anyone who has any experience of depression knows full well that this is virtually impossible. You simply cannot 'snap out' of depression and the negative thinking that is associated with it. It is very easy, in fact, it is the norm, that you will have negative thoughts and this, in turn, makes you think more negatively. Very quickly you can get into a spiral of decline where you are sinking further and further down into a deeper depressive state. It is not nice, but there seems to be only one direction to go and that is spiralling downwards, and the further you go the harder it is to pull yourself up again.

There is hope, though, and a way of managing this, which in time will become very effective and, although it may not in itself treat the depression, it can certainly manage the depression and allow you to lead a much more normal, positive, happier life. What you need to do in the first place is recognise these negative thoughts and stop that spiral of decline taking effect.

The idea is that whenever you start to think negatively or something happens to set you back and put you into a negative mindset, then recognise this, log this, and take action. That action is to go to your toolbox. This is your personal toolbox, which we will develop and fill with different tools, and tailor them to work best for you. It is important to understand that everyone is different and therefore something that works well for someone else may not necessarily work for you.

The toolbox is designed to be a collection of practical applications that you can go to at anytime to find something appropriate that will stop the spiral of decline and pull you back upwards, before negative thinking manifests itself into more negative thinking. The more options you have in the toolbox, the more likely you will be able to find something that works quickly and effectively in any given situation.

Imagine a real toolbox with a variety of tools that are each different but all have their own uses. If you just have screwdrivers, or hammers, or wrenches, then your toolbox isn't going to be the saviour of the day in all situations. However, if you have a full spectrum of tools, then the chances are you will have something there to fix whatever problem arises.

| Some examples of what could be in your toolbox | – feel free to add some more of your own |
|---|---|
| – Listen to some favourite music<br>– Go outside for a walk<br>– Have a long, hot shower<br>– Arrange to meet a friend for a coffee<br>– Go to the cinema and watch a film<br>– Cook yourself a healthy meal<br>– Have a good tidy-up and clean the house<br>– Write down a list of productive things to do<br>– Set some goals and focus on how you will achieve them<br>– Do some gardening<br>– Read some inspiring quotes<br>– Identify some new hobbies or skills to learn<br>– Go to the gym or try a new exercise class<br>– Read some books or do some of your own research<br>– Watch some funny clips on YouTube<br>– Take a short break somewhere for a day or two<br>– Try writing some poetry<br>– Think about doing a charity fund-raising event | |

**CHAPTER 1 SUMMARY**

This has all been about recognising that it will take time and effort to turn your ship around onto a course that will beat depression, but it is possible and will happen. To make sure this happens, you must think more positively and do as many productive and helpful things for yourself as possible. Look forward to how your life will be and use the toolbox to manage the depression and prevent the spiral of decline and block the vicious circle of negative thinking and depression. These small steps are what are needed at this stage, but they will make a big difference.

# Chapter 2

# Reasons, Triggers &

# Understanding Yourself

*Objectives:*

*This chapter is about trying to find some explanations, reasons, and understanding as to why you feel the way you do. There is always an explanation, and the more you understand yourself, the factors, the triggers, and why you react, think, feel, and behave the way you do, then the more you will gain control and be much better placed to deal with, overcome, and prevent those feelings, and therefore beat depression.*

## Working out the reasons and explanations

There are many symptoms of depression and below is a long, although not exhaustive, list. Many of these characteristics you could and would associate with stress and often the line between stress and depression is very blurred. It may be the case that someone does not realise they have depression, even though they may feel stressed and will admit to being overly stressed.

The way people are usually formally diagnosed with depression is by completing a questionnaire asking for symptoms and if they have several of these for a prolonged period of time (usually for a few weeks minimum) then they are diagnosed. Many of the symptoms could be natural and normal reactions to bad news or negative events that occur in everyday life. However, depression is much more than this and will generally see a wider range of symptoms, and the reaction is greater than you would normally, and reasonably, expect.

Take your time to consider this list and I am sure you will agree that none of them are pleasant or wanted symptoms, so it is really important to work out how best to manage your situation so that many of these can be prevented or minimised.

- Being restless and agitated
- Waking up early, having difficulty sleeping, or sleeping more
- Feeling tired and lacking energy, doing less and less
- Using more tobacco, alcohol or other drugs than usual
- Not eating properly and losing or putting on weight
- Crying a lot
- Sadness that does not go away
- Difficulty remembering things
- Physical aches and pains with no physical cause
- Feeling low-spirited for much of the time, every day
- Being unusually irritable or impatient
- Getting no pleasure out of life or what you usually enjoy
- Losing interest in your sex life
- Finding it hard to concentrate or make decisions
- Feeling anxious all the time
- Blaming yourself and feeling unnecessarily guilty about things
- Lacking self-confidence and self-esteem
- Being preoccupied with negative thoughts
- Feeling numb, empty and despairing
- Feelings of helplessness and hopelessness
- Distancing yourself from others, not asking for support
- Avoiding other people, sometimes even your close friends
- Taking a bleak, pessimistic view of the future
- Experiencing a sense of unreality
- Self-harming (by cutting yourself, for example)
- Thinking about suicide

## Understanding yourself

It is very important to try and understand as much as possible about yourself, how you deal with things, how you feel, why you behave a certain way, why you react, why you think the way you do, and what is best for yourself. You need to be responsible and accountable for  yourself and the more you understand, the better position you will be in to prevent problems, manage issues, and overcome the challenges you face. Everyone is different, so you are the best-placed person to really know and understand yourself. As Aristotle said, *"Knowing yourself is the beginning of all wisdom".*

However, understanding and knowing yourself can be much more difficult than it sounds and often requires a lot of work, effort, and time. Just because something works for somebody else that doesn't mean it is right for you. Although it is good to seek advice, you need to be conscious that people are different, circumstances are different, and usually people giving advice don't know all the factors or have all the necessary information or knowledge. You are most likely to be best placed to understand yourself.

Take time to get to know yourself, try to understand your characteristics, behaviours, and personality. Do research, gain knowledge, seek feedback, ask for advice, listen to others, reflect on situations and experiences, learn from mistakes, think about your strengths and weaknesses, and find out who you really are. The more you know yourself, the better you will be able to advise yourself and communicate to others so they can understand and advise more appropriately.

Do this exercise whereby you write down how you feel about yourself and your characteristics, identifying both the positive and good things about you, and also the negative things. Include your strengths and weaknesses. Take some time to think about this and be honest with yourself. Then ask a close friend or family member for their view on you in the same way. It is a good exercise to reflect and see what you think of yourself and to see how someone else views you.

| | Your opinion of you | A close friend or family member's opinion of you |
|---|---|---|
| Positives | | |
| Negatives | | |

Another good exercise to do is think about and write down your current thoughts about the following eight areas of your life so you can identify some key areas of 'good' things in your life and also those areas you currently feel negative about.

| Area of your life | Write down all the positive thoughts you have about each of these areas of your life | Write down all the negative thoughts you have about each of these areas of your life |
|---|---|---|
| Family | | |
| Partner | | |
| Work | | |
| Health | | |
| Friends | | |
| Money | | |
| Time | | |
| You | | |

# Improved toolbox

So from the first chapter you know what the toolbox is and how it can work and be effective. I now want you to continue working on your toolbox by making it bigger and better with more options for you and more that you know will work well for you. It is an individual thing, where some options will work better for some than others, so make sure you tailor yours to what will be best for you.

As well as spending time on adding new tools to your toolbox and identifying those that will work best for you, it is essential that you use the toolbox and practise with those tools. It isalso essential that you recognise any dips, negative thinking, unproductive actions, or general downturns in your mood. The earlier you recognise any of these, then the quicker you can go to your toolbox, pull something out, and stop that dip. You can quickly and effectively pull yourself back up, improve your mood, and stop any potential spiral of decline.

The more you do this, the easier it becomes. You will eventually see it as a very natural, almost automatic, response to anything that might have previously been negative for you. Build your toolbox, use those tools, practise with them, and you will start to feel very confident in being able to manage situations and events on a daily basis and be in control of your emotions, thinking and behaviour.

List some more possible tools you could add to your toolbox—they can be big or small. Let's make it a bigger and better toolbox!

e.g. plan a new business you could set up

– Research where you would go and what would you do if you travelled for a month

– Identify a new sports team you could support and get excited about

– Go for a facial, a massage or a spa session

**CHAPTER 2 SUMMARY**

The second chapter has been primarily about trying to identify some of the key issues as to why you feel the way you do and this is best done by understanding yourself and your circumstances as much as possible. By taking the time to reflect on who you are and what you think about yourself you can better understand the causes and reasons for the depression. This in turn gives you some explanation and that will help to give you some control back over the thoughts and behaviours.

It is still early in the book so don't expect huge progress yet, but be assured it is beneficial and you are making progress – remember seemingly small steps will lead to big gains.

# Chapter 3
# Healthy Lifestyle &
# Managing Stress

*Objectives:*
*In this chapter the focus is on living a healthier lifestyle in general, with a focus on the physical side of things. This is because your physical health has such a key role to play in your mental and emotional health. If you can improve your physical health, you will certainly make a real positive difference to beating depression.*

## Healthy lifestyle

There are so many factors that will affect our health, and by health I mean physical, mental, and emotional health. Some of these factors will be out of our control, but most of them are within our control and we can make a huge difference to our own health by doing more of the right things and less of the wrong things in order to have a healthy lifestyle and thus the benefits that accompany this.

A healthy lifestyle doesn't mean you have to be down the gym for two hours every day and only eat broccoli and spinach! A healthy lifestyle simply means you are aware of what things are good for you and you incorporate them into your everyday life. So yes, that includes exercising and being physically active on a regular basis, and yes, it includes eating plenty of vegetables

and cutting out the sugar. However, it also means reducing your stress, not worrying, taking time to relax, sleeping well, limiting your alcohol consumption, not smoking, smiling more, getting outdoors in the fresh air and countryside, cooking your own meals, and generally making an effort to look after yourself.

| Examples of your unhealthy lifestyle traits | Why is this unhealthy? |
|---|---|
| e.g. Most evenings I have a few drinks to help unwind | Alcohol is a depressant, it's fattening, it can be addictive, and it won't help you to feel happy |
|  |  |
|  |  |

| Examples of your healthy lifestyle traits | Why is this healthy? |
|---|---|
| e.g. I have porridge for breakfast each day | Because it is filling, not filled with sugar and fat, stops me bingeing on unhealthy snacks, and helps set me up for the day |
|  |  |
|  |  |

# The benefits of exercise and healthy eating

'To keep the body in good health is a duty... otherwise we shall not be able to keep our mind strong and clear.'

— Buddha

## Effects on the brain chemistry

We all know that exercise is good for us and can improve our health and make us feel better, yet most of us don't actually know why. The main reason is that exercise makes our brains function at their best. Physical activity is crucial to the way we think and feel, and plays a significant role in regulating and improving our neurotransmitters and bolstering our brain's infrastructure. The brain responds like most muscles do, by growing with use and withering with inactivity. The neurons in the brain connect to each other like leaves on branches, and exercise causes those branches to grow and bloom with new buds, enhancing and improving our brain function.

The brain is of course very complex and much of what goes on is still not really understood. However, it is known that many of our thoughts, behaviours and emotions are controlled by chemicals in the brain called neurotransmitters, and four of the key neurotransmitters are:

**Serotonin** – is responsible for mood, anxiousness, self-esteem, and impulsive and compulsive behaviour.

**Beta-endorphin** – is responsible for modulating emotional and physical pain. It contributes to feelings of self-esteem, euphoria, and emotional confidence.

**Norepinephrine** – affects arousal, alertness, attention, and mood.

**Dopamine** – is vital to movement, attention, cognition, motivation, and pleasure (and addiction).

Ideally, we would all have regulated and optimal levels of these neurotransmitters so we feel happy, well-balanced, and confident, and so that our thoughts, behaviours, and emotions are how we would like them to be and seen as 'normal'. However, for many people this is not the case, and their neurotransmitters are lower than optimal and poorly regulated, leading to a range of emotional and mental health issues, which also affect our physical health.

Exercise and physical activity is a fantastic way of helping to elevate and regulate these chemicals and make us happier, more alert, less stressed, less anxious, more balanced, less reactionary, etc. Our brains will respond very quickly to exercise, and positive results and outcomes can be seen immediately, as well as continued and sustained benefits. Our brains are so important and should be given the respect and attention that is necessary, and the good news is that exercise can be incredibly effective for our brains and therefore our overall health and wellbeing. Do not underestimate what exercise can do for your brain!

'Exercise is a wonder drug that hasn't been bottled.'

Write down here some of the physical activity and exercises you are going to do, starting today and carrying on through the coming weeks – e.g. walking, running, cycling, squash, badminton, yoga, Zumba, football, Pilates, hiking, dancing, circuits, etc. and start planning when you will do them, who you will do them with, what classes to sign up to, what you can do at home, etc. EXERCISE WILL SIGNIFICANTLY HELP YOU!

# Food and Mood

Both directly and indirectly your mood can increase and decrease as a result of the food you eat. A healthy diet will directly improve your mood, helping to boost and regulate various hormones and neurotransmitters in the brain, as well as having a direct benefit to your body, organs, and skin. Indirectly you will feel better about yourself as you will be pleased and proud that you have eaten well and been healthy, further improving your mood, confidence, and self-esteem. This should also help to maintain or even improve your motivation to eat healthily.

If you eat unhealthily then this, too, will directly influence your mood, as it negatively affects your brain chemistry and your body, organs, and skin. You may get an initial 'high' and increased mood from certain unhealthy foods, but then you get the come down and the low is generally worse, and will last longer, than the high. Feeling lethargic, full, bloated, and generally unhealthy will also affect your mood and you are likely to feel worse about yourself for these reasons. A lack of discipline, knowing you shouldn't have eaten that, being ashamed of yourself, beating yourself up about what you have done, etc., are all possible results which are not good and will not benefit you.

Many people will 'comfort eat' for a variety of reasons, but most people who do this are fully aware it is bad for them and they will often feel worse after they have consumed the unhealthy food. The initial comfort soon fades and is taken over by guilt, shame, worse mood, feeling more depressed, etc. The food we consume really does have a huge impact on how we feel, how we behave, how happy we are, what we do, how we are with others, and how we feel about ourselves. In so many ways, we are what we eat, and therefore if we eat well and in a healthy way then we will feel well and healthy, and of course the opposite is generally true, too.

A great idea is to record a food and drink diary and alongside record a mood diary. Write down what you consume and when and how your mood is throughout a day. Do this for a couple of weeks. It is likely you will see some strong correlations between your food and your mood, in both a good and a bad way.

## Alcohol and other vices

Many people turn to alcohol and/or drugs when they are feeling low and depressed as a way to try and cope with the issues and problems they face. In addition, alcohol and/or drugs are often the cause of problems and issues that can result in depression. Therefore, whichever way you look at it there is a strong relationship between alcohol and drugs, and depression or similar issues.

People often turn to alcohol and drugs because they are feeling low: they want to escape from the depression, the problems, and the pain they are facing. They want something that will make things better, a quick fix or to make everything go away and help them forget about their situation. Alcohol and drugs, though, are depressive themselves and will only make things worse.

The very short-term fix and relief and good feeling are heavily outweighed by the longer-term negatives. It is very much like putting a small plaster over a very serious and deep cut. Alcohol and drugs are also addictive and there can be a financial issue with their purchase.

You must also be aware that even if you are not depressed and your life seems OK, this could all change if you become a regular user of alcohol and/ or drugs. There is a high risk of addiction and depression as a result. Either way, you need to be aware of the damage and negative elements of both alcohol and drugs and take action if you feel they are or could become a factor in your life. By understanding the consequences and effects, you are much less likely to fall into the destructive clutches of alcohol or drugs.

# Reducing stress

The official dictionary definition of stress is:

'A state of mental or emotional strain or tension resulting from adverse or demanding circumstances.'

Another definition, which I often use, is as follows:

'A stressful circumstance is one with which you cannot cope successfully (or believe you cannot cope) and which results in unwanted physical, mental, or emotional reactions.'

It is important to recognise and remember that sometimes stress can be a good thing. Often small amounts of stress in the right circumstances can be very beneficial as it can make us more focused, more disciplined, and our adrenaline levels may increase, helping us concentrate and perform to a high level. However, unless controlled and managed properly, stress will usually cause unwanted characteristics and symptoms, which will continue to get worse if nothing is done.

There are many characteristics and symptoms of stress, and, although you would expect many of these to occur as a reaction to a particular event, there is a big difference between stress and a normal reaction to one-off situations. Stress will usually build up, often quite slowly, and the gap between your symptoms at the outset and where they are now is significantly wider, although you may not be aware of how wide that gap has become. Here are some responses by individuals when asked the question, "What symptoms, behaviours and characteristics do you associate with stress?"

- Loss of confidence and low self-esteem. Feeling numb and not valued. Inability to sleep, or tiredness despite a full night's sleep. Loss of appetite or cravings for sugar, caffeine, or alcohol. Irritable and negative thought patterns. Withdrawal from friends generally, even though you previously enjoyed social occasions.

- Anxiety, an overwhelming feeling of being out of control, panic, irrational behaviour. Not having a clear head to deal with the challenges you are facing. Disjointed sleep patterns, loss of concentration and focus.
- Stress can cause many negative and destructive emotions and behaviours. Often a feeling of anxiety, which leads to irrational and runaway thoughts. Tension throughout the body, shallow breathing, excess perspiration, inability to relax, constant worrying and agitation. Being unable to focus on anything other than the tormenting, catastrophic thoughts, leading to an ever-expanding circle of negativity.
- Anxiety, being short-tempered, irritable, and impatient. Not listening to reason, and withdrawal, and having negative emotions.
- Symptoms of stress include poor concentration, anxiety, and lacking motivation to be able to tackle the tasks you face. Behaviours and characteristics associated with stress could be a loss of appetite, having mood swings and snapping at people, lack of sleep, or being unable to sort/prioritise workloads/tasks.
- Feeling overwhelmed and unable to cope with increasing pressures. Getting frustrated, irritable, impatient, upset, and angry. Feeling tired and tense or unable to relax and switch off.

A useful way of looking at stress and the effect it has is by breaking it down into stages. Stress will usually build up over quite a period of time and the person directly affected may not recognise the real damage and risks unless they step back and look at the different stages. Here is a familiar pattern and breakdown of stress:

**Stage 1** – In the first stage you may find yourself feeling overworked, uncertain of your own abilities, but reluctant to take days off.

**Stage 2** – In the second stage you may find yourself tired, irritated and frustrated, working long hours but seeming to achieve less. You may be skipping meals, or comfort eating.

**Stage 3** – In the third stage you may feel resentful or guilty, you will probably be neglecting your family and friends, and will no longer be enjoying work or life.

**Stage 4** – Finally, you may withdraw completely, succumb to illness, or drug or alcohol abuse, feel like a failure, or completely break down emotionally and mentally.

Even in the earliest stages, it is important to recognise stress and seek to manage it and control it as much as possible. It is far too easy, once on the path towards stress, to stay on it and for matters to build up and get worse, and the further down the path, the harder it is to change course. So take time to reflect and think about your own personal situation, your stress levels, and what you can do to manage those effectively.

## What causes stress?

Everyone has a different set of circumstances in their life, with different factors that affect them and different ways of dealing with and managing those factors. A factor that affects one person will not affect another, at least not in the same way, so it is important to understand the differences and apply it to you.

Think about all the factors and areas of your life that you feel create and build stress for you. Write down a list, and then as far as you can, try to put them in order of those that affect you the most and cause the most stress.

Here are some responses from people when asked the question, **"What main things and factors cause stress in your life?"**

- People – partners, family members, work colleagues. Situations – money, health, work, or parenting issues.
- External factors beyond your control like health issues. Work – when people let you down and don't deliver what they say they will, creating more pressure for you. Friends who don't support you as you would hope when you are experiencing a difficult time in your life.
- Money causes stress. Work – too much of it and not enough people to cope with it. Moving home or buying a house.
- Loss of control in personal and work life.
- Financial worries, relationship problems, pressure at work, not having time to exercise or do the things you want to do. People who are rude or inconsiderate and letting you down.

There are a wide range of factors that can cause stress in people's lives and have a negative effect on them; however, many of these factors are very difficult to prevent. So many issues are caused by other people, or events where the individual affected has no control and cannot change the situation. There is so much dependence on another person doing something the way you would like, and when they don't you become more stressed.

So much of your stress and how it causes problems for you is not within your control. Therefore, if you can't change what happens you must try to focus on how it affects you and how you deal with those factors. Remember stress is your reaction to something, so no matter what the 'something' is, you can be in control of how much it affects you and how much damage it causes. You have to learn to manage your reaction to those factors that cause stress.

# Stress-related depression

Generally speaking, if you asked any group of people, whether that was in a work environment or to the general public, if they had ever been stressed or were stressed or even do they suffer with stress, many people would say yes. Often they would laugh about it and say 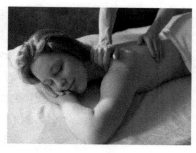 yes, I'm always stressed and life is stressful, who isn't stressed?

The reaction tends to be one of not taking stress too seriously, and people feel relatively comfortable admitting to feelings of stress. It doesn't seem to be something people are ashamed of or embarrassed about, and they will admit to stress.

However, if you asked the same groups if they had ever had depression, were depressed or were suffering with depression, then very often the answers and reaction would be very different. Significantly fewer people would admit to having depression and there would be no laughter or amusing reactions. The general response would be more muted, less admission, and a little bit of unease. People tend not to recognise or admit to depression, often feeling ashamed or embarrassed by the word.

Yet stress and depression are so often linked. Stress can be a major factor in depression and the characteristics and symptoms go hand in hand. A very common form of depression is the stress-related or stress-induced type and it is vital that people recognise this and understand the link. Once understood then it is very possible to manage stress which in turn will prevent depression.

I have learned over the last few years how to manage stress effectively and prevent any depression occurring. I have also learned and understood how the build-up of stress and the way I used to deal with stress-causing factors caused my own personal stress-related depression. I suffered with many of the symptoms of depression without really understanding or knowing what was happening to me or why I felt the way I did. Through extensive research, reading and thinking I understood that I had been exposed to huge amounts of stress, and combined with my type of personality, it was almost inevitable that depression would result.

However, once the strong link between stress and depression is understood, then you can begin to work out the best and most effective ways of reducing stress and managing situations so that you can deal with anything, and depression in this respect is always preventable. The underlying causes may always be there but you can manage the effect and put in place the techniques and use the tools so that you can be 100% confident that depression will never result as a consequence of not managing your stress.

## Curse of the strong

A book I read a few years ago and one I would strongly recommend to anyone who feels they may be suffering with stress-related depression is called *Depressive Illness: The Curse of the Strong* by Dr Tim Cantopher. Essentially the book explains how a certain type of person can become ill from depression caused by stress. That person would usually be viewed by themselves and others as 'strong', the type of person who has great qualities, achieves a lot, whom people look up to and admire, who is determined and successful. In fact, they have many very favourable and welcome characteristics, although in addition they have others that are mentioned below in this list:

**Personality characteristics:**
- (Moral) Strength
- Reliability
- Diligence
- Strong conscience
- Strong sense of responsibility
- A tendency to focus on the needs of others before one's own
- Sensitivity
- Vulnerability to criticism
- Self-esteem dependent on the evaluation of others

So basically, if you are this type of person then you are actually quite vulnerable to getting depressed as a result of stress build-up, and a large percentage of people who suffer with depression fall into this category. A very good way of summing this up is as follows:

Give a set of stresses to someone who is weak, cynical, or lazy and he will quickly give up, so he will never get stressed enough to become ill. A strong person, on the other hand, will react to these pressures by trying to overcome them. After all, he has overcome every challenge he has faced in the past through diligence and effort.

Fill in the table below with examples of things that increase your stress levels on the left-hand side, and examples of things you can do that would lower your stress levels on the right.

| Examples of what causes you stress | Examples of what can reduce your stress |
|---|---|
| e.g. Getting PPI-related phone calls and texts | e.g. Go for a walk at lunchtime |
| Driving – traffic, middle-lane motorway drivers, people who don't signal, too slow drivers, tailgaters, etc | Have a long, hot shower |

**CHAPTER 3 SUMMARY**

This chapter has been about your general lifestyle, particularly focusing on your physical activity, your food and drink, and your stress levels and how you manage them. These three areas of your life can dramatically affect your mood and can both cause depression and feed it, so making it worse. However, a healthier lifestyle with more exercise, better nutrition, and reducing your stress can reduce depression and prevent it coming back.

You can do so much to help yourself in this way by living a healthier lifestyle and the efforts you put in will be worth all the rewards you get from doing those

# Chapter 4
# Belief Systems & The Brain

*Objectives:*
*In this chapter we look in more detail about the way you think, your*
*belief systems, how your brain works, and also your support network.*
*so firstly we focus more on you, and then we look at other help that is*
*potentially available for you to utilise and to further benefit from.*

## UNDERSTANDING YOUR BRAIN AND THOUGHT-PROCESSES

### Belief systems – negative vs. positive

Everyone has belief systems, and they will vary along the spectrum from very negative through to very positive. Although each person will vary and their beliefs will at times change, in general they will have a range they sit in and will therefore be either typically negative or positive.

A belief system is essentially a set of viewpoints and principles on which we base everything we do, feel, think or say, so it makes sense to us and helps us understand what is going on in our lives and around us. We are always receiving new information and seeing new things so to help us understand and process this we compare it to what we already know or believe. The previously stored information is the basis for our belief systems and we anticipate future events based upon our belief systems.

Therefore, having positive beliefs and sitting in the positive belief system range is so much better than being in the negative range. This is because you are more likely to anticipate positive things, look forward in a positive way, and expect more positive things to happen to you. You are far more likely to have experiences and see events that confirm your belief system than the opposite, so you can see what a huge difference your general belief systems can have to your life.

If you have a negative belief system, you will be expecting negative things to happen, so your belief is proven correct and can be reinforced. It's almost as if you want negative things to happen so you can feel like you are right! A negative mindset with a negative belief system will attract negative outcomes.

Here is a table with some examples of negative and positive beliefs – feel free to add more of your own.

| Examples of negative beliefs | Examples of positive beliefs |
| --- | --- |
| I'm not very academic so I will do badly in my exams | If I work hard and put the effort in then I should do well |
| I'm not very fit so I will struggle to do any exercise | I'm not very fit but I can get fit if I start and build up steadily |
| I don't want to fail so I don't want to attempt something just in case I do fail | I don't want to fail but if I don't try, then I will never know if I will succeed and I know I can deal with it if it doesn't work out |
| I'll probably never meet any-one and I should accept I will be on my own for the rest of my life | I might be on my own now but that could change at anytime and one day I will be with the person I want to be with |

For most people going through depression they will have a negative mindset and belief system. That could be due to a combination of many recent negative experiences and events and therefore it is a more temporary belief system or it could be that they have always had a negative belief system based upon their childhood, upbringing and general life events. Their beliefs haven't really changed because they have always been thinking that way and reinforcing their beliefs without really realising it. However, no matter why or how your current belief system has come about, it is possible to change it, and if you can have a positive belief system then it will make a huge difference to your life and play a big role in beating depression.

## Internal vs. external thinking

As well as our negative or positive belief systems, we also have differing ways in our thinking in terms of whether it's internal or external. Again, there is a wide spectrum, from extremely internal to extremely external and everything in between, yet we will all fall somewhere within this range.

Generally speaking the more internal your thinking is, then the more confident you will be and you will feel more powerful and be more in control of your life, which has to be a good thing. The more external your thinking is, the less in control you are. You will often feel powerless and lack confidence, which will generally have a negative impact on your life.

If a person has a strong internal way of thinking, they will believe that can usually control or strongly influence their life in terms of their experiences and what will happen to them, and also be able to deal with anything that has happened to them. They feel more powerful, responsible, and in control, and this thinking increases confidence.

On the other hand, if a person has a strong external way of thinking then they will think that their life and experiences are more often than not controlled or strongly influenced by external factors such as other people, luck, fate, God, etc. This way of thinking is often disempowering and will most likely reduce confidence. They feel they don't have much control or influence over events, or their life in general, and everything happens to them as a result of outside factors and influences.

| Examples of internal thinking and behaviours | Examples of external thinking and behaviours |
|---|---|
| I passed my driving test because I put in lots of practice and I really focused. | I don't know how I passed my driving test, it must have just been a lucky day and the examiner was feeling generous. |
| I didn't get that promotion at work but the other candidate was really good so I now know what I must do and work on so the next time I will. | I didn't get that promotion at work. It's not fair and I'm always unlucky. There's no point even trying. |
| I need to try to get fitter so I'm going to enter a 5km event, set out a training plan, and then get going. | I need someone else to help me get fitter as I just can't get motivated and do it on my own. |
| I'm hiking up a mountain at the weekend and the weather forecast doesn't look good so I better make sure I have my waterproofs. It will be more of a challenge! | I'm hiking up a mountain at the weekend and it's just my luck that the weather forecast is rubbish. Why does this always happen to me? Well, I will cross my fingers and hope it won't rain too much. |

The more you can have an internal way of thinking and thus feel more powerful, more in control, more influential and more confident over your life and what happens, the better. It will significantly help in the fight to beat depression.

If you are relying on luck, or other people or some kind of greater being to come and rescue you and make your life wonderful, then the chances are not much will change. If, on the other hand, you can become

more internal in your thinking, then you can have much more direct influence on your life and be more in control.

Make a real effort to dismiss anything that is external and instead focus on what you can do yourself to have more power and influence over your own life.

## The Chimp paradox

A book that I would strongly recommend is *The Chimp Paradox* by Dr Steve Peters. He is best known for being the team psychiatrist for British Cycling and Team Sky, helping the likes of Sir Chris Hoy, Sir Bradley Wiggins and Victoria Pendleton. The book is described as a mind-management plan and tries to explain the different ways the brain works based on neuroscience principles; this in turn helps explain the different thoughts and behaviours we have. By understanding why we think and behave in certain ways it is then possible to be more in control of our thoughts and behaviours in order to reduce any anxiety and increase our confidence, happiness, and success.

I will try and explain the basics of the book and hopefully this will be helpful. However, reading *The Chimp Paradox* in full is advised for a clearer insight.

In simple terms, the brain is divided into three areas that Dr Peters describes as the Computer, the Human and the Chimp, which are all very different.

Starting with the Computer, this is the part of the brain that is full of experiences and memories built up throughout your whole life and will include both good and bad experiences. Nearly every thought and subsequent action will be based in some way on your past experiences, and therefore it is important to understand the significance of those experiences and that you can change how they affect you in a positive way. If you have had bad experiences in your life, then the likelihood is that they will continue to have a detrimental effect on you long after the actual experience. You may not be aware of or realise the damaging effect they can have, but these 'gremlins' are likely always to be there unless you can address them by recognising them, understanding them, and then getting rid of them!

## Example of a gremlin

Imagine being a ten-year-old at school, when the teacher asked a question of his pupils, you put your hand up and answered in front of the class. However, you misheard the question and your answer was very wrong. But worse than that you had simply given a wrong answer was that the rest of the children started laughing out loud and even the teacher laughed at you. You felt incredibly embarrassed and upset and that feeling haunted you for ages. Ever since, you have become reluctant to speak out, answer questions, or put your view across, for fear of this embarrassment happening again. You continue throughout your life being very wary and reluctant to speak up and your confidence is affected as a result.

Now let's look at this rationally and see if we can get rid of this gremlin.

Firstly, we all make mistakes and get things wrong. Secondly, you were only ten years old and the children who laughed were only ten years old – you would have probably done the same. Thirdly, you misheard the question, which wasn't your fault. Finally, it was just one incident when you were very young – you cannot let this affect you anymore. Acknowledge it happened and then rationally dispose of this gremlin. That situation will not happen again, so speak up, answer questions and you will regain confidence in this area.

Hopefully you will also have had good experiences and these are likely to continue to play a positive role in your life. Of course, the more positive experiences, the better and it is important to recognise these as well as recognising the negative gremlins. The positive experiences are referred to as 'auto-pilots' and the aim is to increase the number of these by generating new positive experiences and also changing some of the bad experiences into positive ones, which can be possible.

The Human part of the brain is the real you, and when this is active and working well then we are rational, logical, calm and mature, and our thoughts and behaviours are based upon facts and our core values. This is how we would want to behave most of the time and how we would want other people to behave. The human part of the brain has developed over hundreds of thousands of years and distinguishes us from other animals. Humans need purpose and fulfilment in their lives.

The Chimp part of the brain is at the core; it is the original part of the brain that existed before the human part developed and grew through evolution. When this part of the brain is active our behaviour can be very 'unhuman', and our behaviours and thoughts are very much how we might expect a chimp's to be. They will be very emotive, reactionary, and impulsive – the main instinct being survival, with the options of fight, flight, or freeze. So in this mood with the chimp in control we could be aggressive, excitable, anxious, scared, naughty, etc. We are not rational, we don't look at the facts, we are not logical, and we are not mature.

## Example of chimp and human behaviour

Let's imagine that you are going to an important meeting which is taking place at 2pm, and it is normally a 30-minute drive or less to get to the location of the meeting. You decide to leave at 1.15pm to give yourself plenty of extra time to get there for 2pm. However, on the way there is some unexpected traffic, a combination of roadworks, temporary traffic lights, and a broken-down car. You start to feel agitated and annoyed, especially as nobody seems to be doing any actual roadworks and you expect it was the person's fault who broke down, causing the additional delay. You have given yourself some extra time, though, so you should still make the meeting on time. Once you are clear of the roadworks and traffic lights you then get stuck behind a really slow car and are not able to overtake. Your frustration builds and you become angrier and even more annoyed. You start to think you are going to be late for your important meeting.

Still stuck behind the slow car, you decide to try a shortcut and drive through a housing estate, but quite soon, with lots of cars parked on the road, you have to stop to let an oncoming car go by. You stop and wait and let the car go by, but they do not wave to say thank you or acknowledge you in any way and you are outraged. You get so angry that you are fit to explode. You can no longer concentrate on the meeting because you are so worked up that you are late and people are so rude, and you finally arrive still angry, upset, and agitated.

It is clear that you have been in chimp behaviour mode! As a result of events and other people's actions out of your control you have let your chimp take over and make matters worse for you. You are upset and angry, and potentially the important meeting is compromised as a result. Now if you were able to manage the chimp and have the human remain in control you would be in a much better position.

You would rationalise that you did allow plenty of extra time to get to the meeting and what happened was out of your control and you are not to blame. You would rationalise that there are always 'idiot' or 'rude' drivers out there but you cannot do anything about that. You would rationalise that the best thing for you would be to stay calm, not get upset, let it go, reassure yourself that it's not the end of the world, and gain some perspective on the situation. You would apologise for being a few minutes late and explain the new traffic lights and roadworks and remain in the right mood and frame of mind for the important meeting.

The human remains rational, calm, and logical whilst the chimp gets agitated, angry, upset, emotional, and reactive. In this situation it is clear that it is better for you for the human to be in control and the chimp to be managed.

The important initial step is to recognise when you are thinking and behaving in Chimp Mode. If you ask yourself the question or reflect on the situation it will be fairly obvious whether you are in Human or Chimp Mode. If you then recognise you are indeed in the latter then you have to work out how best to manage this and how the human can regain control. If the chimp's behaviour and thinking are around anger and aggression then it may be best to allow the chimp to have a short outburst, but then quickly put him away in a cage to calm down. If the behaviour and thinking are more about being worried, anxious, and scared, then it may be best to reassure your chimp, give him or her a hug, providing protection and security.

Here is a simple chart explaining some of the key differences between the Human and the Chimp:

| | HUMAN | | CHIMP | |
|---|---|---|---|---|
| **Behaviours** | Logical   Rational<br>Level-headed<br>Gets the Facts<br>Mature | | Reactive   Irrational<br>Emotional   Excitable<br>Anxious   Aggressive | |
| **Life is all about...** | Purpose   Fulfilment | | Survival | |

## No. 1 rule – Life is not fair

Unfortunately, it is true to say that life is unfair. So often things happen to us and other people, both directly and indirectly, that are not fair. It is not nice and is not right but it is fact! The sooner you accept that life is not fair, the better. Often in life, when negative things happen, there is nothing to blame or it is nobody's fault: it just happens and we have to move on and get on with improving our lives and doing what we can do.

## Inner troop is very important

Your inner troop refers to those people that are closest to you and who you can trust, feel supported by, and depend on, and where there is a mutual respect. Those people who are positive for your life help you to be a better person, lift you up when needed, and are honest and truthful with you. Now you may expect that from all your family and friends; however, this is not always the case and too often you will find there are people in your life that do not fit the above description. These people have a negative effect on you and your life, and wherever possible you need to get rid of them!

It is far better to have quality than quantity with your inner troop and it is important you make a real effort with these people, too, to maintain and enhance the relationships of the troop. Drop those that are not good for you and have a negative and damaging impact on your life if you can. Remember it is your life and you can drop those people who cause issues and, although not easy, it will make your life better. Your inner troop is very important to your happiness and confidence.

## You can only do your best!

A further important message from *The Chimp Paradox*, that also impacts on confidence, is the fact that you can only ever do your best. You cannot do better than your best – that's not possible. So whatever the situation or circumstance, if you have done your best, you should be happy, as you cannot possibly do any more. Therefore, no matter what the result or outcome is, be positive and proud that you have done your best. By doing your best, that is fantastic and a wonderful achievement, and that should give you more confidence.

## Identifying and managing the chimp

Practise identifying your Chimp and Human behaviour and also other people's. Every day you will find yourself both in Chimp Mode and in Human Mode – when you make a concerted effort to recognise your behaviour it is usually very clear what mode you are in.

When you find yourself in Chimp Mode try to understand why – ask yourself these questions:

- What events, actions, people, circumstances, etc. have made you act, think and behave in Chimp Mode?
- Has being in Chimp Mode helped you?
- Has it made things better for you?
- Do you regret anything you did or said whilst in Chimp Mode?

Developing techniques to manage the chimp and allow the Human to take over:

**Step 1** – You have to first recognise you are in Chimp Mode.

**Step 2** – Remind yourself that in most cases being in Chimp Mode will not be beneficial for you.

**Step 3** – Try to take a step back or a deep breath and think what a mature adult human would most likely do in that situation.

**Step 4** – Think how best to manage the chimp in that particular situation. For example, does it need reassurance? Does it need to let off steam? Does it need to be put in a cage?

**Step 5** – Remind yourself again that you are the human and can manage the situation and take control of the chimp.

Write down some examples of when you are in Chimp Mode and Human Mode – what do you do or say?

| Chimp Mode examples | Human Mode examples |
| --- | --- |
| e.g. you hold the door open for someone and they walk straight through completely ignoring you and no mention of a thank-you and your chimp is outraged! How dare this person treat you as if you weren't even there and be so rude! Your chimp feels like running after them and punching them in the face! | The human recognises that some people are rude, are inconsiderate and have no manners. You realise that getting upset and angry and reacting this way will not help or change anything. You try to let it go and forget about it as quickly as possible so it has a minimal effect on you. |
| | |
| | |

# YOUR SUPPORT NETWORK

## The right people around you

Having the right people around you can make a huge difference to how you are able to deal with life's challenges. On the other hand, having the wrong people around you can significantly hinder any progress, and indeed, they may have contributed to the difficulties in the first place.

Generally speaking, humans are sociable animals and like to spend time with other people, so it is normal that people like to have friends and people around them who they can talk to and spend time with. It is important, though, not to hang about with people who can have a negative effect on you and probably are not real friends. Be careful not to be brought down by others or used by others in any way. It is better not to have friends than to have people around you who will have a negative and damaging influence on you.

If you are lucky enough to have good people around you – friends and family – then make sure you appreciate this and utilise their friendships in a positive way, especially if you need some support. Talk to them and explain how you feel, as they will want to help. They may not be able to help or know what is best but they will have your best interests at heart. If you feel that people close to you are not in a position to help or give you the support you need, then there are alternatives.

There is a lot of support available if you look for it and ask for it, but it is unlikely to find you unless you make the effort and be proactive. Find experts or people with knowledge and experience so that you are more likely to receive the information, advice, and support that will be most beneficial.

Get rid of people who bring you down and cause you issues and embrace those who genuinely care for you and have your best interests in mind. It is never too late to make new friends and have the right people around you and in your life.

'There comes a time when you have to stop crossing oceans for the people who wouldn't even jump puddles for you.'

## Professional help

Many people find it hard to ask for help for a number of reasons. They may feel they have failed, they may not want to burden others with their problems, they may feel that nobody would understand or be able to help, or they may not feel worthy of someone's help. However, it is very important to seek help, and that can come in many formats, including professional help. Do not be afraid to go to your doctor and tell them how you feel. Stress and depression are very common and are recognised problems. Seeing your doctor should be part of the process of recognising the issues, managing them, and then overcoming them.

Doctors are busy, they may not have much time to see you, you may not feel comfortable seeing them, and you may feel, because you don't see the problems you are experiencing as a physical illness, that it doesn't merit a visit to the doctor – but you should go. Talking is beneficial, as is seeing what professional advice is available to you. It could be help with sleeping, or possible treatments for depression like medication, counselling, or cognitive behavioural therapy.

You are entitled to professional help and your doctor should be the first port of call. The earlier you do something, the easier and quicker the solution. If you keep putting it off then it is likely that the symptoms and effects will only worsen. Do not in any way see it as a weakness to speak to your doctor about your troubles, as it is much more of a strength to admit there are issues and then to tackle these in the best way possible for yourself, your family, your friends, and your colleagues.

'Asking for help is a sign of strength, not weakness'

## Medication

Many people take medication, such as antidepressants. In fact, the numbers have been growing significantly over the years, and continue to grow. Many people also have certain views on taking medication, which on the whole are based on ignorance rather than facts and appropriate information. The more knowledge and information on medication you have, the better placed you will be to have a relevant view that is not based on ignorance.

Medication has been around for many years and vast improvements and changes have been made over that time, with a wider variety now available. Generally, there can be side effects with medication and they will usually take a few days, sometimes weeks, to become effective. Sometimes they are not effective at all for the individual. Everyone is different and, although medication will not work or be right for some people, if a doctor has recommended it then you should certainly consider taking it.

Do your own research, try to understand what the medication is supposed to do, be aware of the side effects, and ask questions. The more you know, the more likely you are to receive the best and most appropriate medication for you. For example, one of the most common antidepressants on the market is Prozac, which primarily targets the neurotransmitter serotonin, as this is known to have an effect on your mood and behaviour.

There is also a risk that if the medication is beneficial and you feel better that you then stop taking the medication too early, which can then bring you right back down again. So always discuss it with your doctor, follow the guidelines, and understand as much as possible about how they work and how they should be taken. Medication can be a life-saver and many people have seen fantastic results, so do not dismiss them, but be aware of the downsides and always look at a range of treatments and ways to help yourself get better.

## Counselling

Talking to a counsellor or psychotherapist may be another option or a complementary option alongside other help. You may be fortunate to be referred on the NHS by your doctor for free counselling, although unfortunately there is often a waiting list. Or you may seek private counselling where sessions can range typically from £30 to £75 per hour.

Several counselling sessions are likely to be needed over a course of many weeks and possibly several months, so you must be aware that the benefits can take time and patience is needed. However, counselling can be a very effective form of treatment, particularly to understand more about yourself and how factors have affected your thinking, feelings and behaviours. You may need to discuss matters from the past in depth that are uncomfortable and upsetting, but this will help you to overcome your current issues and allow you to be happier in the long run. You may also feel worse initially before you feel better, particularly with psychotherapy, as things are discussed and understood, so be aware of this possibility.

There is a risk that the counselling isn't effective for you, perhaps because you are not ready to open up and talk, or the counsellor you have is not right for you. There is some luck involved in being matched with the best person for you, and many people try a few before really finding the great benefits that are possible. So do not feel deflated and demoralised if counselling doesn't work for you initially. Look for other options and be patient if you can. Also, if money is a factor then try to look at the cost of counselling as an investment in your future and your future happiness.

As always, the more you understand yourself and the issues you are facing, the better placed you will be to get the right help and for the treatment you choose to be effective. So do not just rely on a counsellor for all the answers; work with them, look at other treatments, and do as much for yourself as you can with the increased knowledge you have from your own research.

## Support groups

If you are feeling low and lacking in motivation then the most important person to change that around is you. However, it is extremely difficult to do it on your own, so it is very important to seek help and support. This support can come from many different sources and in many different ways. Everyone's circumstances are different so you need to look at what support is available and what is likely to work best.

The support from family and friends may be sufficient, but often that is not enough or it isn't available in the first place. Be open-minded about the support that is available and do some research and investigation to find out the opportunities. It may be that your employer is able to offer support, so explore those possibilities, too.

You may try local support groups or local charities and organisations that can provide beneficial support and help. It could be you could get free counselling or cognitive behavioural therapy if you look into this. There may be Internet forums or groups that can provide help and support. The best way to find out is to research and talk to people. Don't be afraid to ask for help and advice.

Most towns and cities will have local organisations detailing charities, support groups and information. Your local library could be a useful starting point. Also ask your doctor if they have any further information or places to refer you to. And of course if you have the Internet you will be able to find a lot of useful information and help there.

## Family and friends

Everyone will have different circumstances when it comes to family and friends, but generally they are going to play quite a big role in helping you deal with, and overcome, challenges that life throws at you. There is a common expression that you can't choose your family, and many people are not close to their family, do not see them often, or do not have any close family.

If you do have family then do not underestimate them and the role they can play. Although you may argue, fall out, disagree, etc., there is usually an underlying love and support there which is unconditional. Do not push them away, but where possible talk and meet with them and use their support, as you would help them if the roles were reversed. If you are struggling then they can be your comfort, offer security, kindness and love, particularly when you are feeling low and alone. They might not understand, they may frustrate you at times, but they will want to help where they can.

If you do not have close family then try not to dwell on this or use it as a negative. There could be many reasons for this position but don't allow it to add to your problems. Instead, accept it and look for other people to be supportive and who can help. Friends can play a big part in your life including when you are struggling, but be aware that you need to communicate and let them know how you are feeling, otherwise it will be difficult for them to understand and help. They may not understand what you are going through even if you do tell them and they may well be having troubles of their own. They may not know what to say or do for the best, and at times will say the wrong things and friendships will be tested, but the benefits of friends will always outweigh the possible negatives.

Be careful about offloading too much onto one person and be careful who you can trust, which will be difficult as you are likely to feel more insecure if you are going through a difficult period yourself. Try to be pragmatic and show empathy, be honest and patient, but do talk and listen to your friends, as bottling things up and trying to deal with them on your own is always much harder.

## Mentor

If you are, or have been, lucky enough to have a mentor in your life, then you may appreciate how beneficial they are and what an important role they can play. It could be one of your parents or another family member, perhaps somebody at work, a teacher you have stayed in contact with, a friend or somebody who has been assigned to you in some way. No matter how you have come across them, having a mentor in your life whom you can confide in, you can trust, you can get advice from, you can bounce ideas with, who will look out for you and what is in your best interests, who can understand you and help when needed, is a wonderful thing.

However, many people will not have and probably have never had a mentor in their life and therefore have not benefited from all the positives they can bring. It may be very difficult to find someone who can be a mentor, but it is something to consider looking for as the rewards can be so great.

Think about whether there is anyone who comes to mind who could be a mentor, and if you can think of someone then ask them if they would consider that. They are likely to be flattered by you asking and willing to take on that role as best they can, but even if they decline, or it doesn't work out, then you haven't really lost anything from trying. If you cannot think of anyone, then try researching possibilities, speaking to people you know to get their input and see if they have any suggestions. You can also consider some of the many organisations, groups and charities that may offer such services.

It may take some time to build the relationship and to get the rewards from it, but I strongly believe that having a mentor in your life can give you something extra, something positive, some additional security, some guidance, some additional support, more strength, and increased confidence.

**CHAPTER 4 SUMMARY**

This chapter has focused on your thinking, beliefs, and behaviours plus your support network. There has been lots to think about and to understand and recognising how important it is for you to have positive beliefs and internal thinking. The *Chimp Paradox* is a great book and model to understand which can be applied every day of your life – but again as with so many other things the more you practice the easier it will be to recognise and manage the chimp behaviour. Also, we looked at how important your support network is and how this can be improved and utilised effectively.

# HALFWAY

## Where is the ship heading?

You should be noticing some improvements with the knowledge you are gaining and working on some of the techniques and utilising your tools. Remember that you will undoubtedly have some bad days during this whole process but the key is that overall you are on the up and building momentum. Take some time to reflect on what you have achieved so far and write down below some of the positives from the last few chapters.

| What things that you are doing are working? | Why do you feel they are working? |
|---|---|
|  |  |
|  |  |
|  |  |
|  |  |
|  |  |

# Chapter 5

# The Many Other Factors

*Objectives:*
*In this chapter we take a look at lots of other factors to consider that may have a direct or indirect influence on you. Read through each one and think carefully about whether these factors do play a role in how you feel, think, and behave. By understanding as much as possible about yourself and the factors that may affect you, you will be in a stronger position to regain control and steer your ship how you want to.*

## OTHER FACTORS TO CONSIDER

### No magic wand

Something that must be understood is that there is no magic wand that will miraculously make everything better. Often people are so focused on finding a magic wand, looking for a shortcut, hoping someone or something will just come along and make everything better.

You have to be patient and realistic. If you focus on trying to find a magic wand solution to your problems then you will neglect all the things that really can help you. It is likely that you will need to focus on several different factors, many of which will have connecting links to each other, but if one isn't right then it will impact on another. So you need to work out and identify as many of those factors as possible, and then understand how to fix these as fully as you are able, rather than just going for a quick-fix, short-term solution.

If you really do want to feel better, be happier, get over the difficult period, feel more confident, and move forward in a positive and productive way, then it will require time and effort as well as understanding. Don't be tempted by shortcuts and quick-fix solutions if you want long-term benefits.

## Your reaction

How do you normally react to things? It is often too easy, especially when hearing bad news, to react quickly and without time to really think. Life will always present problems, and obstacles will be put in your way, but it is usually how we react to these that will have the real impact on how we feel and cope and to what extent we are affected. Particularly when feeling low or depressed we tend to react very quickly and focus on the negative aspects of any unwelcome news or events. This does not allow us to think in a clear and controlled way and we are less rational. What may be a relatively minor problem can become a much more difficult problem as a result of our reaction to it.

Although it can be difficult, the best advice is to try and be more pragmatic and allow some time to pass so you can absorb and digest the information before reacting. This may require effort and practice to be able to become less reactionary but the rewards are worth it. By taking more time and getting some perspective on the news you hear or the barriers that have been placed in your way you will be better equipped to handle the situation and you significantly reduce the risk of overreacting and making the situation worse.

Learn to be more measured, more pragmatic and more patient in any response and you will find yourself being able to cope better with any situation. Imagine a boxing match where you are taking some punches and struggling to deal with them. You are better off defending these punches, soaking up the pressure to give yourself some time and regrouping before hitting back. If, instead, you decide to start swinging wild punches back, leaving yourself wide open, then there is a much greater chance that you will be knocked out.

# Control

There are so many things that affect our lives every day and have an impact on the way we feel and behave. No matter who you are or what your situation is, it is inevitable that there will be instances each day that you are not happy with, do not like, or do not agree with, and that will affect you in some way. The important thing, though, is about how you deal with those instances and how much you allow them to affect you.

So many of the things that happen to you each day that annoy you or upset you are out of your control. You could not and you cannot do anything about it as you don't have the influence, power, or control to change it. It is not your fault, yet you are being affected by it. That is not fair, it is annoying, it is upsetting, but that doesn't mean you have to let it affect you. Remind yourself that you could not control what happened, there was nothing you could do about it and there is nothing you can do about it, except focus on letting it go and not letting it affect you.

Here are a few examples where you may feel angry or upset:

- The person who does not acknowledge you in the car when you stop and let them by.
- The person who doesn't say thank you when you hold a door open for them.
- The person who doesn't signal correctly at a roundabout.
- The suicide bomber who kills loads of innocent people.
- A friend's cat getting run over in the road.
- The only cash machine in the area is empty just when you need cash urgently.

• The massive traffic jam on the motorway that means you are late for an important meeting.

None of these are within your control and you just have to accept that these things happen and try not to let them affect you. They are not your fault, you cannot change them or control them, so just let them go and focus on those things that you can control or change for the better.

# ARC

Think about all the things that happen regularly, possibly daily, that annoy you, upset you, and cause you stress. Although, in and of themselves, they may not cause depression or other illness, they can have a major impact on your mood, happiness and quality of life. There are so many examples of things that affect you and can cause problems or make underlying issues much worse.

Doing the shopping, dealing with bills, commuting to work, people you work with, cold-calling, customer service centres, bad drivers, long journeys, traffic jams and form-filling are all examples of everyday things that can cause issues. However, there is something that could be helpful, called ARC, which stands for Avoid, Reframe, or Cope.

The idea behind ARC is that for anything that causes stress or similar problems, then ask yourself, at first, if you can possibly avoid it. If it is possible, then do exactly that: avoid it, so you are then not affected in that negative way. If, however, you cannot avoid it, then ask yourself if you are able to reframe it or change it in any way so that it is less harmful, upsetting or negative for you. If it is not possible to avoid it or reframe it in any way, then you have no option but to cope with it. However, understanding and recognising the negative impact, and knowing that you are just going to have to cope with it, can actually reduce the stress and the issue quite a bit and therefore be more beneficial.

An example might be food shopping. It may cause all kinds of issues over parking, lack of trolleys, being too busy, long queues, you may have kids with you causing problems, etc. and you may dread the whole thing, causing stress beforehand as well as during the shopping. Unfortunately, food shopping cannot be avoided as you need to eat and have food in the house and feed the family. But can you reframe it? Could you go at a time when it is less busy and stressful? Most places have supermarkets that are open 24 hours these days. Could you go without the kids? Could you use Internet shopping and home delivery instead? If for any reason you find yourself in a position where you have to go shopping on a busy Saturday afternoon, then you will just have to cope. You know it will be busy, it will be noisy, there will be queues and it will be stressful, but you are aware of this and will get through it and you will cope. With that mindset things won't be so bad and it will not have such a negative effect on you.

## Feeling sorry for yourself

One of the most common things that people do when they are feeling low and depressed and struggling with life's challenges is to feel sorry for themselves. It is a natural emotion and reaction when things are not going well, when life seems so unfair, when everything seems against you, and when you feel so fed up and low about everything. Nevertheless, moping around, with your head down, focusing on all the problems and feeling sorry for yourself is not going to make things better. Nothing will change if you continue to feel sorry for yourself, and as hard as it may seem you must focus your efforts on productive actions and thoughts.

From time to time when everything seems too much, having a moment of feeling sorry for yourself and, perhaps, even shedding some tears, can be helpful in that it will release some emotion and pent-up anger, frustration and pain. A short crying session can be a good thing. However, if you spend a lot of time feeling sorry for yourself, dwelling on all the negative things, then you will be facing a much longer recovery process than necessary.

Understand that, although feeling sorry for yourself is a symptom of depression and feeling low, you have the control over this and by focusing on productive actions you will deal with and overcome the issues more

effectively. Whenever you find yourself in that state where you are feeling sorry for yourself, tell yourself that it is not helping and won't make things better. You may get a little sympathy from people to start with, but that will soon go and will not help you get through this difficult period.

Look for positive, productive things to do and things that will take your mind off those issues that are causing the stress and pain.

## The blame game

When something goes wrong or something doesn't go the way you would like it to, then it is all too common for people to look for something or someone to blame. It's as if there must be blame attached to something or someone, otherwise how could it have happened (or not happened). You may even blame yourself. But why do we do this? Why do we have to have someone or something to blame for anything that affects us in a negative, upsetting or unfair way? We don't seem to be able to move on unless we have attached blame. There seems to be a real need for us to find the reason, or the excuse, for something and therefore blame can be given. So what is wrong with that?

There are two fundamental wrongs here in relation to the blame game. The first is to put blame onto something in a negative, unproductive way. There is little room for understanding or for learning from the experience. Saying it is his or her fault, or that was to blame, is a one-dimensional, emotive reaction from which no one benefits, even if it is true.

Secondly, have you ever heard the phrase 'shit happens'? Well, this is the real world we live in and in life shit does happen, and often there is no person or no thing that is to blame. Things go wrong, negative stuff happens, things won't go according to plan or how you expect them to, and life will throw us a curve ball. However, that does not mean there needs to be blame attached. You can accept the situation for what it is and move forward without all the negativity and unproductiveness of the blame game.

## Envy and jealousy

It is very easy to become jealous of someone and be envious of someone else's position or their particular circumstances. They have this or that, they look like that, they have money, they have the job, they have the car, they have the house, they have the partner, etc. – a never-ending list of how someone else has it better than you. Now if that list was genuine and then you were able to use it in a motivational, aspirational, inspirational, positive way, then being jealous might have some benefits.

However, it is much more likely that nothing positive will result from envy and jealousy. It will make you bitter, angry, upset, and negative. You will be looking for excuses and reasons and blaming others as to why you don't have those things you want. You will become resentful and make false assumptions and poor judgements based upon envious and subjective emotions. Envy will have damaging and longer-term effects. It will eat you up, making you a jealous, bitter, negative person who will naturally dislike people, seek to blame others, and feel the whole world is against them. Well, life might not be fair, and you may have some bad luck and others some good luck, but envy and jealousy are very negative emotions. Nothing good can come of them and the sooner you get these damaging, destructive emotions out of your life, the better.

If possible, whenever you feel yourself getting jealous, try to let that emotion go. Remind yourself that it is of no benefit to be feeling like that and having those thoughts. It is negative, non-productive, and potentially harmful. You don't have to be pleased for them or have any emotion towards them, just ensure that you don't have any negative, jealous thoughts yourself that will affect you. Just let it go.

Once you have learned how to let it go, then you can feel in control of this harmful, negative emotion that is jealousy. It will no longer control you and have those damaging effects on you. You can rise above it and move forward with your life in a more positive way. Being in control of this then allows you, if you like, to turn other people's perceived good fortune and success into a more positive outlook for yourself.

Ask yourself why you perceive them to be fortunate and successful. Digging deeper into this area allows you to understand what you perceive success to be and allows you to think about what you want and what your aspirations might be. It may provide some goals, targets and ambitions and you can use this as motivation to start achieving some of these. However, along that journey you may also find that many of the things you were previously jealous about are not actually that important after all and your perception of fortune and success is different in reality.

## Assumptions and judgements

We spend so much of our time making assumptions and judgements both of events and of people, and much of this is necessary and natural. However, we often make unfair and incorrect assumptions and judgements, which can cause issues both to ourselves and to other people. You have heard the expression, "don't judge a book by its cover" and you will be aware that you shouldn't make judgements without having all the facts or hearing both sides to the story, but that doesn't seem to stop us. In addition, when we are going through our own difficult times it seems that we tend to make even more assumptions, and make judgements that can be unhelpful, damaging, and potentially destructive.

Making negative assumptions and judgements about events and people is increased and connected to being more paranoid and having lower self-esteem. This in turn causes more paranoia and concern that lowers self-esteem further and makes us think up even more negative and unhelpful assumptions and judgements. It is a vicious circle and difficult to get out of, unless you recognise what you may be doing and act upon that.

Try not to make assumptions or make judgements unless you are confident you have all the facts and a full understanding. Chances are you do not. Try to find out more or not think or worry about it at all. Do not feed your paranoia with negative possibilities and focus on unhelpful and unproductive scenarios. Instead, try focusing on things that will increase your self-esteem and reduce the paranoid thoughts and have a much more open mind. You might not be able to control what other people do and think, but you do have a choice over what you do and think.

'Before you assume, learn the facts. Before you judge, understand why.'

## Comparisons

In a similar way to being envious and jealous of others we often create issues or make issues worse by comparing ourselves with other people, particularly people we know, whether that is family, friends, work colleagues or our peers. Many people spend much of their time comparing themselves to others, which is generally a very unproductive and negative thing to be doing. Only if the comparisons can help you focus, work harder, and inspire and motivate you to better things can it be beneficial. Usually, though, comparisons are made in a negative way.

Firstly, everybody is different, and in so many ways, therefore you will never be able to compare like for like. Secondly, you are very unlikely to ever have all the facts and information, so comparisons are always built upon assumptions and judgements and we have previously mentioned the issues with that. Thirdly, comparisons nearly always make you focus on the things you don't have as opposed to the things you do have.

People have different abilities, different talents, different capabilities, all with varying strengths and weaknesses and mixed with different circumstances, timing and luck, so you just have to accept that like-for-like comparisons are not possible. Just because someone, in your opinion, has a better car than you or is better-looking or has more friends or has more money or has a bigger house or is smarter or is healthier or is more confident or has more luck, etc., that does not really mean anything. It is your perception and your opinion and you do not know all the facts involved, and so what anyway? Focusing on those sorts of comparisons is damaging and is much more likely to reinforce negative attitudes and beliefs and be unproductive than do anything positive for you. Try comparing less and focus more on what you have and the positive elements in your life, rather than thinking or worrying about what other people have or don't have.

# Habit

You may feel like you are always having to deal with problems or you are always unhappy or always feeling depressed or stressed. You may constantly be moaning about things, seeing things negatively, focusing on the low points and feeling sorry for yourself. Things may seemingly always go wrong and everything seems like hard work, and you crave sympathy and want people to see your struggle.

There is a possibility that your depression has become a habit. You have become conditioned to feeling like that and it has become the norm for you. You have allowed these thoughts and feelings and behaviours to become a habit and the more it has become a habit, the more difficult it is to stop.

Humans are quite good at having habits of all different kinds because we get used to things and become set in our nature. Depression and feeling low can become a habit. We become used to it: the feelings we have, the way we see things. The way we act and react to situations can all become habitual. You have become used to things going wrong, you expect that to happen, you are used to being unhappy so you are not expecting to be happy, and in a way you feel uncomfortable and uneasy if things are good, and you are feeling happy because that doesn't feel right.

The good news is that habits can be kicked into touch. You can change, and the habit of feeling low and depressed can be removed. But to kick this habit you need to recognise that it is a habit that you can overcome and effectively be a much happier, positive person as a result, and start getting used to that and make being happy a habit.

'We first make our habits and then our habits make us.'

## Accountability and responsibility

In a similar way to the position in which people always seem to want someone or something to blame if anything goes wrong, people are generally pretty poor at accepting responsibility or taking accountability for things. It is all too common for people to pass the buck, say it is nothing to do with them and let it be someone else's problem.

You need to be accountable for your actions and decisions and take personal responsibility for the position you are in. You may be in a dark place, you may have made mistakes, you may have a mountain to climb in various ways, but in order to move forward, to learn, to be happier, and to climb that mountain you must have accountability and take responsibility yourself. You are the most important person in all of this and you cannot go through life shirking responsibility and hoping things will turn out OK.

Do not bury your head in the sand and pretend the situation doesn't exist. Be honest with yourself, understand the position you are in, don't hide away, take responsibility and that way you have the best chance of dealing with any situation or circumstance. You may not like the position you are in, but it will only get worse if you ignore it and don't face up to the situation and don't seek appropriate help and support. It takes a stronger person to be honest and face up to things than to ignore them and you can be that strong person. The sooner you do, the sooner you will be dealing with the issues properly and constructively, meaning that you will overcome them more quickly.

## Feedback

Something that many people are not particularly good at is giving and receiving feedback, whether that is at work or in our personal life. Generally, people are reluctant to give feedback that is deemed negative or what should be called, more appropriately, constructive feedback. And if they do provide this feedback they are often poor at communicating it effectively and delivering it in a constructive way that will lead to improvements and benefits for all parties. An even bigger problem than giving feedback is how poor people are at receiving feedback that isn't what they want to hear.

Any sign of criticism or anything deemed negative will often make people go very defensive straight away. They can stop listening, put the barriers up, look for excuses, look for blame elsewhere and often become so unreasonable that it becomes impossible to have a sensible and constructive discussion. This reaction is of no benefit to either party, particularly for the person receiving the feedback, so in nearly all cases their reaction makes everything worse.

Being able to give and receive feedback is a skill and should be something that people can work on and get better at. Being able to take constructive criticism and feedback, listening to the points being made and having a sensible discussion is much better than putting up the defences, not listening, and not accepting that possibly you have made a mistake or could have done something different or better. We are all human, we make mistakes, we are not perfect, and we can learn from others and learn from events and actions.

The skill of empathy is very relevant with regard to feedback and the ability not to react. You may disagree, you may be right, but it is important to listen, discuss and communicate first before forming a view and making assumptions about what someone is saying. You will be better off if you are able to receive and give feedback in a constructive and fair way.

'Be open to criticism but don't be affected by it. Criticism is meant to help you be a better person. Learn from it.'

## Don't be too critical of yourself

If you find yourself in a position where you feel you are struggling and not coping with what life is throwing at you, it is quite possible that you blame yourself. You may feel like you are failing and it is your fault that you are in this situation. You may have a partner and family you feel responsible for and think you are letting down. You may feel that you have not met your own expectations, and as a result become critical of yourself.

Perhaps you have made mistakes, you could have done better, and many of the problems you face have been caused by your actions and decisions. However, remember that everyone makes mistakes and it is likely that many of the actions and decisions were made with the best intentions and you didn't have the luxury of hindsight. Putting yourself down and being self-critical is unlikely to help matters.

You are probably being very unfair on yourself, and if it was somebody else in your position you would take a much more sympathetic and less critical view. Give yourself a break and realise that you should treat yourself, as you would treat others, with less criticism, less negativity and less blame. A more positive attitude and being nicer to yourself will be far more beneficial both for you and others close to you.

'We have to learn to be our own best friend because we fall too easily into the trap of being our own worst enemy'

## Patience

One of the key factors in dealing with life's challenges and overcoming difficult situations is understanding the need to be patient and recognise that things will take time. Patience really is a virtue and can be critical in being able to deal with a wide range of problems. People will naturally want things to get better as soon as possible and will be keen to end the emotional pain they experience. However, this lack of patience can cause more problems if you are not careful.

Anxiety, stress, and paranoia can increase and depression can worsen if you try to rush things and not allow the appropriate and necessary time to recover or deal with the issues you are facing. As mentioned before, there is no magic wand and things will inevitably take longer than you may wish to get better, but patience is a strong and very important factor in overcoming the difficult times and issues you are facing.

Learn to be more pragmatic, don't be afraid just to wait if you are not sure what to do for the best, and accept that things will take time. In the long run it is best to deal properly with issues rather than just trying to gloss over them and hope you will be OK. If, for example, you are taking medication or seeing a counsellor then it will take time to see and feel the benefits, potentially several weeks and months. If you have suffered a loss or a relationship break-up, been involved in a traumatic event, or are suffering with depression, then it will take time to deal with those issues properly and overcome them effectively. Another expression, "time is a great healer", is also very relevant and true, as the mind and body need time to deal with the issues, so although it may not seem like it, things will improve, you will feel better and the pain you go through will go away.

'Patience is not the ability to wait, but the ability to keep a good attitude while waiting.'

## Empathy

In order to be able to help other people, one of the most important skills to have is empathy. It is also a very important skill to have in order to help deal with your own problems and prevent them occurring in the first place. Empathy is being able to see the situation and understand it from the other person's point of view. It is also a skill that is not given the attention it deserves and generally people are not good at empathising effectively.

If you are depressed or struggling to cope with issues then it is very common yet also very deflating when you try to  explain how you feel to someone and they just don't understand. Often people will never understand because they cannot relate to the issues or don't have the appropriate experience associated with the problems. However, often it is because they do not try hard enough to empathise and understand. If someone tells you their problems or asks for help try as much as you can to show empathy and understand their position.

If you are struggling then it is important that you empathise, too, and don't jump to conclusions regarding what somebody says or does. Put yourself in their shoes, try to understand why they have done something or said something, rather than making assumptions which will generally be negative ones. If someone doesn't seem that helpful or understanding don't immediately think they don't care or they can't be bothered or they think you are being silly. Instead, think about it from their viewpoint, as it is far more likely that they do care but are not sure what to do or say for the best.

## Don't think everything is OK too soon

Everyone will go through bad experiences and difficult times and feel low during their life. This is natural and normal and, unfortunately, life will always provide challenges and obstacles. Many people, however, will also suffer from depression and a prolonged period of feeling low with additional symptoms and factors affecting them. If you are going through a period of depression, you must understand that it is only temporary and things will get better, especially if you seek the right kind of help and do things to help yourself.

However, there is a danger that once you start to feel better or have a good couple of days you make the mistake that everything is OK. Please don't make the mistake that everything is OK too soon. You feel better so you stop doing the things that helped make you feel better again. If you stop doing the things that were helping, then there is a risk that you could sink back into depression. For example, it could be that you stop taking medication, stop exercising, stop reading helpful books, stop talking to people about the problems, stop eating the healthier foods, stop taking the breaks you need, etc., and if that happens you could end up back where you started.

Keep working at feeling better, learn which things helped you feel better, do more of the positive, productive things and realise that you want to feel good again for the long term and not just a few days. It is great news if you do start to feel more positive and better: just be aware that everything might not be OK just yet, so be prepared to keep putting in the effort and the rewards will be much longer-lasting.

## Your past

By definition you cannot change the past. It has happened, it has gone, and it is history. Yet it affects all of us, all the time and in many ways. To a large extent the past shapes us and we are who we are today because of past events and circumstances. This can be in a positive way and you may have had a fantastic childhood and upbringing, great parents, great friends, done amazing things, and be very happy with how your life has gone. However, very often this is not the case. Things have happened in the past that affect you in a negative way and you hold onto these so that they continue to affect you going forward. Why do you allow this to happen? You cannot change the past, but you can change the future. Though no one can go back and make a brand new start, anyone can start from now and make a brand new ending.

Don't let the past hold you back. If it is negative, then let it go. Look forward and be free of those chains that tie you to the past. You have the power and control to break free of those chains. It is your life and you shouldn't let anyone else have a negative, damaging effect on you. You cannot change the past. However, if you feel that it is too difficult to just forget about the past and not think about previous events, circumstances, people, etc., then you need to dig much deeper and really understand why it is causing such problems. Why are these historic events causing issues and holding you back? You may need professional help for this if you cannot understand and find those answers for yourself. It is much better to go through some difficult emotional pain in the short term, which may happen, if it means you get your life back and can move forward free of those chains and negative emotions.

Common examples of past events that can cause so many problems include your childhood and family issues with parents, family break-ups, siblings, stepparents, etc. You may have been abused physically and emotionally, bullied, unloved, shown no affection, and misunderstood. Of course, these will naturally cause effects and issues but you need to understand and believe that you can be in control as to what extent you allow this to affect you. The reality is that none of this is your fault. There is a good chance that a lot of this was nobody's fault. There are usually fundamental reasons why people behave the way they do, and whether it is right or wrong it is often not their fault. For example, if someone has bullied you or abused you, it is more than likely that they were bullied or abused themselves. It doesn't make it right but it does give some understanding. So once again, there is an issue here over blame. Be careful not to blame someone for the sake of needing to assign blame. Understanding is a far greater, more powerful, and more positive route to take.

I know people who have had bad childhood experiences. I myself went through many difficult times as a child, but although it inherently has an effect on personality and behaviour, I have managed to let the past go and not let it hold me back. I have tried to understand, not seek blame, and I feel free of whatever chains could have been tied to me as a result. Many people have not been able to do that. They blame the past, they blame individuals from the past, they look back at the past, they use the past as an excuse, they live the present and the future alongside the past, and as a result they are held back.

## Guilt and no sense of worth

For many people who struggle with depression there is a feeling of low self-worth that worsens as the condition gets deeper. There is a feeling of guilt, sometimes shame, and a view that they don't deserve to be happy or don't deserve to be given help and support. They may feel guilty for causing any problems or somehow not living up to certain expectations they have placed on themselves or perceive to be put on them by others.

These thoughts of guilt and low self-worth are usually a result of childhood experiences and they have developed and become deep-rooted as the person goes through life. Perhaps they were told they weren't good enough or couldn't achieve things or weren't allowed to take part in activities. Having people tell you that you can't do something or you are not good enough, especially from those close to you, will undoubtedly have a long-lasting negative effect.

If you feel that sense of guilt and low self-worth, then it is important to try to understand why and what events or experiences or people have made you think like that. It is very likely that the people who said those things to you had their own issues and as hard as it is to ignore or forget about those past events you need to realise that this is not your fault.

Nobody has the right to make you feel like that and it says a lot more about the person making the remarks than it does about the person receiving the comments.

You no longer have to feel guilty; you are worth something and you can be worth so much more. The past has gone and you can choose to ignore it and not let it affect you once you understand that those experiences were not your fault, and it is your life for you to live your way.

## It's not your fault

Many people who suffer with depression or struggle with life's challenges blame themselves and believe it is their fault. It could be that other people have told them this or suggested it throughout their lives and so they assume it must be their fault. Most people who have experienced some kind of physical or mental abuse during childhood have the underlying belief that it was their fault and they are to blame for what happened to them.

A traumatic event out of the blue could be the reason or a major factor for your feelings and behaviours, which nobody could have predicted, and certainly was not your fault. Life is full of events, some good, some bad, some tragic, which can have different consequences and effects.

Also, you could be more likely to suffer with depression due to genetics, which, of course, is not your fault, yet without knowing this you could make the assumption that you are fully to blame for the way you feel. There are usually clear reasons for the way you feel and behave that are a result of many factors, events, and people in your life and this is not your fault.

You won't be perfect: there will be things you could have done and can do, but if you are suffering and experiencing turmoil then it is likely you are not to blame. Do not make the assumption that it is your fault.

Lift that weight from your shoulders, that burden of guilt, that sense of unworthiness, so that you can move forward in a productive way.

## Not everything is possible

You will often hear quotes that talk about anything being possible, and if you want something enough then you can get it and nothing is impossible. Well, although that thinking can often be beneficial and motivating and can help people achieve much more than they would have done otherwise, there are dangers. Sometimes you have to accept that some things are not possible and that you cannot achieve everything you want. You are only human, and despite all the motivational quotes, the reality is that not everything is possible and if you keep trying then you may end up paying the consequences. Real strength is knowing when enough is enough and having the courage to stop and accept that you simply cannot do everything, and some things, no matter how much you want them and how hard you try, are just not possible.

Many people can become ill and very unhappy by trying to take on too much and achieve too many things. The pressures, responsibilities and stresses can build and the increasing sense of desperation and looming failure when the impossible is not being achieved all combine in a very negative way. Fighting not just an uphill battle but also a war that cannot be won has the potential to be very dangerous for your health. You must know when enough is enough and accept that not everything is possible.

That doesn't mean you should stop believing, hoping and dreaming. The possibility that you will be happy and will achieve what you want is much more powerful when you can accept that not everything is possible. There is nothing wrong with dreaming what it would feel like to win that Olympic gold medal, to climb Everest, to land on the moon, to become president, to play at Wembley, to star in that movie, to be the boss, etc., even though you accept that they are not possible for you. Possibility is all about hope, and without hope then life can be very empty. So possibility is everything – just be aware that not everything is possible.

'Not everything is possible; but possibility is everything'

# Trust

Putting your trust in someone can be very difficult, particularly if you have had your trust broken in the past, and you may feel scared, vulnerable and reluctant to take a risk in trusting people again. However, going through life without someone to trust in and confide in can make you feel very lonely and encourages you to bottle feelings up and not express yourself. You must be careful about whom you trust, and it is sensible to be cautious, particularly around sensitive and personal matters, but don't automatically think that nobody can be trusted: you must be prepared to let your guard down.

Trust should be developed so be careful not to rush into a relationship, friendship, or partnership expecting high levels of trust straight away, as it takes time to get to know somebody and feel comfortable and safe in opening up to them. Not everyone can be trusted and you may get let down and hurt, but your life will be much better and more fulfilled if you are able to trust a close group of friends or family so that you can share feelings and feel secure in doing so.

Although it will be natural to have your guard up if you have been hurt and let down with trust in the past, do not let other people and past experiences stop you from forming trusting relationships going forward. Communication is key to trust as well as not making assumptions, and just like anything worth having it will take time and effort to develop.

# Honesty

It is, of course, important to be honest, both with yourself and with other people. Honesty is essential to good relationships and friendships and being honest with yourself is paramount to your own happiness. However, particularly if you are struggling with issues, you may start to distort the truth, be in denial, not mention things, or even lie outright. This could be because you don't want to admit the truth or believe it, you may feel embarrassed or ashamed, you don't want others to get hurt in any way, you may feel unworthy or feel like you are failing. You may put up a front, cover the truth up, pretend things are OK and lie about the situation you face.

However, as the saying goes, "honesty is the best policy". Being in denial is of no benefit, covering things up will only make them worse, lies will ultimately get found out and you are risking not getting the support and help you may need by not being honest. Once you start lying it can be a difficult path to get off and you are likely to lose people's trust, lose friendships and relationships, and your own self-esteem and view of yourself will only worsen.

Be strong enough and brave enough to be honest with yourself and with others, as this will always be the right thing to do no matter how hard it may seem at the time. What would your view be of someone who was dishonest? Even if their reasons were because they were struggling with challenges in their life you would have much more respect for them and would want to help and support them if they showed honesty.

# Worrying

Most people worry too much about things and people who suffer with anxiety, stress and depression in particular spend much of their time worrying. On the whole worrying is a negative and unproductive behaviour which is unlikely to help matters and most likely to make you feel worse. Of course, if you are considering things in a productive, structured way and perhaps planning how best to deal with them, then this is beneficial, but it is different from worrying.

Ask yourself if you really need to worry about whatever it is that is concerning you. Is it really that important? Have you got it in perspective? Have you made assumptions that could be wrong? What would happen if you stopped worrying about it? Also, it is common to worry about things that are way ahead in the future, yet you can spend all that time in the build-up worrying. Is it possible to wait and not worry until much closer to that event or situation, thus saving yourself so much additional stress?

It can be helpful to talk to others and discuss what and why you are worried as this may help you get a different perspective or the specific help or support that is needed, and if nothing else then you have released some of that built-up negative, stressful emotion. Alternatively, if you cannot talk to anyone, then write the problem down on paper and try to articulate why you are worrying. This will help you see things more clearly and be much more constructive than just worrying in your head.

'Worrying doesn't take away tomorrow's troubles, it takes away today's peace.'

'Worrying is like a rocking chair, it gives you something to do but doesn't get you anywhere.'

'Worrying will never change the outcome.' 'Most of the things you worry about never happen.'

# Fear of failure

Nobody likes to fail at something or feel like a failure, but it is an inevitable part of life, so what is important is how you deal with failure and how you can learn from these experiences in a positive way. So many people fear failure and as a result spend much of their time worrying about it. In addition, the fear of failure stops people doing things that could result in positive outcomes, achieving things and being happier.

First of all let's focus on the worrying part around the fear of failure. If you spend your time thinking about the negatives, dwelling on what could go wrong and being scared of what failure will mean, then the chances of failing increase. You can reduce the risk of failure, work on plans to increase your chances of success and be sensible and realistic with activities and challenges you face but do not fear failure. Instead think about the positives, stop worrying, and your chances of success will increase.

If you let the fear of failure stop you from doing things then you are limiting your chances of being successful. Even if you do fail at something, you should look at it as being one step closer to success, because each failure is a stepping stone to where you want to get to. Learn from failures and from the experience so you become more knowledgeable and a stronger person. You may get hurt, you may feel upset and you may feel as if you have taken a backward step but often to go forward you need to first of all take that step back.

Everyone who has succeeded has always failed, so do not fear failure. Accept that it can happen and most likely will but do not let it stop you from living your life and ultimately reaching your goals and being successful. Read the following quotes and take some time to think and reflect about your view on 'failure'.

'Failure is not the opposite of success. It's part of success.'

'Success is not final, failure is not fatal; it is the courage to continue that counts.'

'Don't worry about failures, worry about the chances you miss when you don't even try.'

'In order to succeed you must first be willing to experience failure.'

'Failures are part of life. If you don't fail you don't learn.

If you don't learn you'll never change.'

'We learn from failure not from success.'

'Those who try to do something and fail are infinitely better than those who try to do nothing and succeed.'

'I've failed over and over again in my life and that is why I succeed.'

'The greatest glory in living lies not in never failing but in rising every time we fall.'

## Fear of rejection

Just about everyone has fears of some kind and, although the fear of failure is probably the most prevalent, the fear of rejection is close behind and in many ways is very similar. Nobody likes to be rejected, whether that is in the context of someone you would like to be with, somebody you have had a relationship with, a job that you were after, or anything where you want it but get rejected. You may not understand why you were rejected and may not be given any reasons, which makes it worse since you start to make all kinds of negative assumptions. You are likely to have your confidence knocked, and dwell on the 'what if?' 'if only', and 'why not me?' scenarios.

The fear of rejection and any past experiences of rejection are likely to prevent you from trying things in the future, and it may seem preferable to keep your barriers up and not go for things so that you will then not risk getting rejected and hurt. Yes, you may not get hurt, but also you may miss out on wonderful opportunities, experiences, relationships and happiness.

It is also about how you deal with any rejection you may face and whether you allow it to hold you back or whether you accept it for what it is and then move forward. You need to decide whether the risk of rejection is greater than the rewards of happiness. An example might be the saying: "It is better to have loved and lost than never to have loved at all".

## Nervousness

Many people suffer with nerves and anxiety. Being nervous is a natural reaction to certain situations and can be a good thing by making you focus and concentrate more. However, for many people nerves can take over and have a negative effect, causing much distress and/or stopping them from doing things that would be beneficial for them. If you find yourself in a situation where you are feeling nervous and it is uncomfortable, particularly if you are worried about what other people might think of you and that they will see you are nervous, then remember the nervous face exercise.

The nervous face exercise works if you go to a mirror and pull four facial expressions. Firstly, pretend you are happy, positive, and smiling and see what that looks like with your facial expression. Secondly, pull a face that shows you are sad, upset, and very negative and see what that looks like. Next, pull a face that is surprised and shocked, and note what that looks like. Finally pretend you are nervous and pull a face that shows your nerves and observe what that looks like.

What you will notice is that with the first three expressions happy, sad and shocked faces – it is very clear to see your emotion. The facial muscles clearly indicate the emotions and feelings you have and other people will be able to see clearly how you are feeling. However, with the final face, showing you are nervous, there is no facial expression. It is effectively expressionless, with no clear sign of emotion or how you are feeling, pretty much blank. So how can anyone determine from a blank, expressionless face that you are nervous? The answer is they cannot and therefore if you are feeling nervous and worrying about what other people will think and will see you are nervous, then remember they cannot tell.

So the next time you are doing a presentation, going for an interview, at a networking event, going on a date, etc. and feeling nervous then be reassured that other people will not notice or be aware, so hopefully this will help your nerves and prevent the nervousness being too much of a problem.

## Financial stress and money

Another consequence of modern life is the importance of money, or rather the importance we place on money. Of course, money is important, but there is far too much emphasis placed on money in our society and as a result this leads to more financial issues and financial stress than should ever be the case. There are many factors surrounding money and the problems it can create, but a lot of the cause of the stress is lack of financial education and too many comparisons along with financial envy and jealousy and the view that money will make you happy.

Many people have financial stress and money problems, usually in the form of debt or money they owe. They do not have financial security, they have that burden of debt, they cannot do things they may wish to, they feel restricted, their options seem limited, and most decisions they make are connected to their financial position. In addition, many people focus so much time and effort on trying to make money and believe that this will make them happy and is more important than anything to the detriment of so many things that are actually more important and could make them happier. Finally, there are people who are in the fortunate position in which they recognise that money is important, but they don't allow it to take over their lives and have the stress that money can bring because they are able to focus more on other things in their life.

'Too many people spend money they haven't earned, to buy things they don't want, to impress people they don't like.'

## Sugar

Something else that can be both a cause and effect associated with depression and feeling low is sugar. For many people sugar is like a drug and people are effectively addicted to it, yet the effect it has on how you feel, think, and behave is often ignored or not understood.

Sugar is more likely to make you tired and feel lethargic than give you energy, and with tiredness come several negative symptoms such as being short-tempered, having poor concentration, irritability, lacking enthusiasm, lower motivation and drive, as well as just feeling low on energy. High sugar intake can also lower some of the essential brain chemicals that affect our mood and how we feel, such as serotonin.

Moreover, an effect of lower serotonin is higher cravings and a reduced ability to say no to those cravings. So it becomes a vicious circle whereby you crave sugar and are unable to say no, therefore take in high quantities of sugar, which actually makes you feel worse, which in turn makes you crave more.

Look at your sugar intake in both food and drinks and see if you can reduce your levels. The recommended daily intake is approximately 30g so this should be your target. Many people will take in at least five or six times that amount without really realising it by eating foods with a high sugar content such as cereal, cereal bars, low-fat yoghurts, low-fat muffins, chocolate bars, baked beans, sugar in tea or coffee, fizzy drinks, fruit juices, etc.

Most things that say 'low fat' tend to have high sugar content, so beware. Make a food diary and see exactly what you are eating and drinking and the associated sugar content. Sugar really can affect your mood and the way you feel, yet you are able to control what you eat and drink so you will have a much better chance of feeling better if you know the effects of what you are doing or, in this case, eating.

## Sleep

We all need adequate sleep in order to function effectively both physically and mentally. Lack of sleep is a very common problem and can lead to many more issues. However, of course getting good-quality, and enough, sleep is easier said than done! There is also the possibility of having too much sleep and not getting out of bed for long periods.

We are creatures who need a certain amount of fuel (food and drink) and a certain amount of sleep and rest each day in order to function effectively. We may be able to go a few days with little food or sleep, but very soon we will suffer consequences if we do not give our body what it needs. Although everyone is different and requires different amounts of food and sleep, we need to understand what our own bodies require.

If you are having difficulty sleeping then start with a basic diagnosis of what could be causing this problem. For example, stress, worry, alcohol, depression, partner, bed, light, etc. Then look at the basic things that could help and are practical, such as reading before sleeping, a relaxing bath before bed, cutting out alcohol, meditation, ensuring your bed is comfortable, not sleeping or napping during the day, a regular sleep routine, etc. Do not underestimate the need for good-quality sleep, and the effects it can have if you are not sleeping. Feeling tired both in body and mind is not pleasant and will make you more irritable, short-tempered, unable to focus or concentrate appropriately, have an effect on your diet, lower your mood, and make dealing with life's challenges even harder. Therefore, take action and you will see and feel the benefits.

'The best way to see what tomorrow brings is to sleep through the night.'

## Back to basics

So many of the problems that we often have to deal with, and the stress and depression that commonly occur in our lives, are effectively self-inflicted due to the modern life we lead. All the pressures, responsibilities, deadlines, stresses, expectations, etc. together with the poor diet of processed and high-sugar foods, and not forgetting the lack of physical activity, contribute to the problems we face.

One of the best things you can do is to try and go back to basics as much as possible. Try to strip out as much of the self-inflicted stresses, try to eat basic, natural foods and try to get out in the fresh air and do some exercise. Focus on the simple things and the basic things, give yourself a break and try to avoid or eliminate so much of the negative, unimportant baggage that drags you down in life. Think 'back to basics.'

You are a human being, an animal who has survived and thrived for hundreds of thousands of years and who has done this with what you would view as the bare basics. Humans are not designed to eat the modern diet of high-sugar, high-fat, processed foods, and we aren't designed to sit about doing no exercise. We are also not designed to stress ourselves out by placing so much pressure on ourselves, having constantly to make decisions and think at all times. We need rest in both body and mind, but we need to exercise and to eat naturally.

If you focus on going back to basics and stripping yourself of many of the negative, destructive elements of modern life, then you will feel better and you will survive and thrive just like your ancestors did.

---

**CHAPTER 5 SUMMARY**

As you may be realising there are many factors to be aware of and consider when it comes to depression and your thoughts and behaviour. This chapter we have looked at many of these potential factors and you should think about how they affect you and to what extent. Everyone will be different so some factors will resonate and be more influential than others but make sure you are as honest with yourself as possible. You may want to go back and re-visit some of them to ensure you understand as much as possible.

You are doing great and I know it is not easy but I guarantee this is working and the effort you put in will be rewarded.

# Chapter 6
# And Still More Factors

*Objectives:*
*This chapter is a continuation of the many factors to consider. Again, like with the previous chapter, read through and think carefully how each one might affect you or be a factor in your thoughts, feelings, and behaviour.*

## OTHER FACTORS TO CONSIDER CONTINUED

### Stop putting things off

How often have you said you are going to do something positive and then not committed to it or implemented it? For example, starting a new fitness regime, losing weight, eating more healthily, learning a new language, sorting out the garage, getting in touch with old friends, visiting a relative, reading a particular book, gaining a new qualification, helping a charity, reducing your alcohol intake, or stopping smoking.

Do you make New Year's resolutions that within a few weeks or months mostly become redundant? Or have you had the same goals and targets for many years without achieving them or perhaps never even attempting them?

Why do people keep putting things off when they know that it will be beneficial, positive and productive for them and for others? It is too easy to make excuses and think it doesn't really matter, or you will do it at a later date and this can become a habit. But think about the rewards and the benefits and the sense of achievement and pride if you stop putting things off and get doing instead. You can become one of those people who gets on with things, does what they say they are going to do, doesn't make excuses and then reaps the benefits of those actions.

Positive actions will increase confidence and self-esteem and you will become more motivated to do even more. So stop delaying and putting things off, and like the Nike slogan says, Just do it!'

Complete the table below with various different things you should do and now will do!

| What are you going to commit to doing? | Why will this be good for you? | When will you do this by? |
|---|---|---|
| e.g. I'm going to clear out the spare room and sort out all the paperwork | Because I hate the mess and clutter and all the paperwork everywhere, and the room is currently a waste of space, so I could use it much more constructively and perhaps even have friends to come over and stay | I will commit to complete this by the end of next weekend |
| | | |
| | | |

# Find a passion

Do you have a passion in your life? Is there something that interests you, excites you, something you look forward to doing and are happy to put some time and effort into? By definition, if you have a passion then you feel passionate towards that activity, and if you feel passionate then you feel alive. If you have nothing that you feel passionate about then it is harder to feel alive and your life will feel less fulfilled and when things get tough you will feel emptier and have less motivation to get through.

It is horrible to feel empty, to feel like there is no point in anything and to feel that life is just too hard, without any enjoyment or happiness. Usually in these situations where people feel empty they have lost their passion, and the emotive, positive feelings that being passionate brings are no longer there.

You need to find that passion again by either returning to a former activity that you were once passionate about, or seeking new passions:

- Try a new sport
- Follow a football team
- Take up cooking
- Learn a language
- Go travelling
- Start drawing, painting or writing
- Read more
- Learn to dance
- Play a musical instrument
- Join a gym
- Learn to ski
- Sort out your garden
- Do some DIY
- Volunteer for a charity

- Get a dog
- Collect some stamps

'Never underestimate the power of passion.'

# Motivation and effort

It can be difficult to motivate yourself at the best of times, but when you are struggling with life's challenges or suffering with depression then finding the motivation and putting in the effort to do things becomes much harder still. It can be so difficult to find that motivation you need to do something or even just to keep you going, and it seems so much easier just not to do anything, even though you know that is not the answer.

So how can we improve our motivation and how can we then make more effort to do the things that are going to help us?

Well, we need to find the ways and methods that will work for us and recognise that we are all different, so what may work for one person may not necessarily work for another. There are many things that you can do to help get motivated, and a good start is to try and understand the benefits of what you are trying to motivate yourself to do, as this in itself should be motivational. If it is something physical then it might help to do the activity in a group at a set time so you are committed to something and other people may help keep you motivated, and the social aspect may be an added reason for going. It is far more likely that you will attend an organised group session at a specific time that you have committed to than just leaving it down to "I'll go and do something myself at some time."

Focus on the outcomes and what it will feel like if you make the effort. Visualise the benefits and feel the positive effects to help give you that determination and desire to help yourself. You could use motivational and inspirational quotes, or real-life examples, so you are more likely to make the effort. Ask friends or family to help or support if necessary, especially in the beginning, as things will become easier once you build some momentum. The more effort you make and more motivated you become, the more you will benefit from what you are doing, and this will make you even more motivated.

It can also be helpful for your own motivation if you can try and help motivate others. For example, you may struggle to exercise on your own and put in the effort, but if you say you will run with a friend to help them exercise and help motivate them, then you are going to benefit just as much, so both people win.

## Sense of achievement

There are few better feelings than a real sense of achievement. Feeling proud of yourself, others feeling proud and pleased for you, being congratulated, knowing the effort was rewarded, reaching a goal and putting a big smile on your face. Yet how often do we have that feeling? When was the last time you really felt a sense of achievement in something? Why don't we do more things that give us the opportunity to have that sense of achievement?

There are so many things that you could do that would give you that sense of achievement and the associated benefits; feeling good about yourself, boosting your confidence and self-esteem, feeling worthy, something to talk about with pride and the positive memories that you can always carry with you and hold onto. It could be something academic, a qualification, a new skill, or perhaps some kind of physical challenge like running a marathon or climbing a mountain. It could be a very individual thing or something you do as a team or in partnership. Think about what you would like to achieve and before you say you couldn't do it, think about and visualise what it would feel like to achieve that. Don't let fear of failure or lack of confidence stop you from at least thinking about it, researching it, asking people about the possibility, and focus on how you can do it, rather than why you can't.

The chances are that unless there is effort, hard work, and commitment, you will feel no sense of achievement but the more effort there is, then the greater the satisfaction and that wonderful sense of achievement. Think about what you could do, and the chances are you can do it. And of course, you could always do a challenge, as that would be a fantastic way of having that amazing sense of achievement.

## Past successes

When feeling low and having to deal with current stresses or periods of depression, it is easy to dwell on the negatives and feel like you have failed. It is common to think that you are a failure, that you haven't achieved anything, you aren't where you want to be in life, and that you are no good at anything. Thinking like that and viewing your life as a failure is not going to help the situation. Although it is difficult, try to concentrate on things that you have achieved in your life, and focus on these past successes. You have achieved things. You have been successful. Remember the things you have done, whatever they may be, and think about them with a sense of pride and accomplishment. It could be exams that you have passed, qualifications you have achieved, job promotions, physical activity achievements, overcoming illness, helping someone else, reaching a personal goal, etc. There will be lots of things that you have succeeded in and things you have achieved. Reflect on these and believe that you will achieve things once more and will have that warm feeling of achievement again.

| List some of your past achievements and successes here: |
| --- |
|  |

Once you start to think about past successes and realise you have achieved things in your life, you can then start to think about future successes and things you want to go on to achieve. Try to get into the mind frame that you want to succeed and you want to achieve, and set some small, realistic goals to start with. Hopefully you can get some motivation and a desire to start achieving again and taking hope from the fact you have not failed and you can succeed.

## Count your blessings

The section about feeling sorry for yourself emphasised the fact that this was unproductive and negative and as far as possible should be avoided. One way of helping to stop those feeling-sorry-for-yourself thoughts and emotions is to think about what you do have and to 'count your blessings'.

It is often difficult for people to understand the pain and horrible feelings associated with depression, especially as it can be an invisible condition where people don't see the real effect and symptoms in a tangible, obvious way. However, so many people feel low and let things affect them too much because they don't have a real sense of perspective on things. Do you have a home, do you have food to eat, do you have all your limbs, can you see, can you hear, can you move about, do you have family, do you have friends, do you have a job, do you have freedom to get about, do you have access to medical treatment, do you have clean water to drink, do you have a television to watch, etc.?

You may have been through terrible times and experienced horrific things, including some of the following (if you have, you are not alone, and if you haven't, then think how lucky you actually are): Have you been abused (mentally, physically or sexually), has your partner been killed, have your children died, do you have a terminal illness, are you blind, are you living on the streets, are you unable to feed yourself, are you in a wheelchair, etc.?

It is very easy to get consumed by your own problems and issues and to lose a sense of perspective, but every now and then take some time to reflect and think about what you do have going for you, and count your blessings. When you see films shown on Children in Need or Comic Relief or adverts for Save the Children, Cancer Research, Oxfam, etc., that should help you get a sense of perspective and realise that actually you are lucky and have a lot of good things going for you. We all need reminding of this from time to time.

'Count your blessings, not your troubles.'

## Comfort zone

You would have heard the expression about being in your comfort zone, and by definition you feel comfortable in this position, which can be a good thing. Feeling secure, more confident, more relaxed, and thus more comfortable is a good place to be. It is certainly a good place to be when we are feeling at our most vulnerable and lowest state. However, the risk is that we never leave our own comfort zone and therefore miss out on so many potential opportunities and other ways that could make us feel happier and benefit us a lot more.

If we never step out of that comfort zone and experience new and different things, meet new people, go to different places, try other activities, etc. then we may be missing out on so much and our lives will be less fulfilled. And the really good news is that nearly always when you step out of your comfort zone and try something new then you will be glad you did. It will be beneficial, better than expected, or at least certainly nowhere near as bad as you thought. And even on those rare occasions when you don't like the experience, you can be proud that you gave it a go and can learn from it in a positive way.

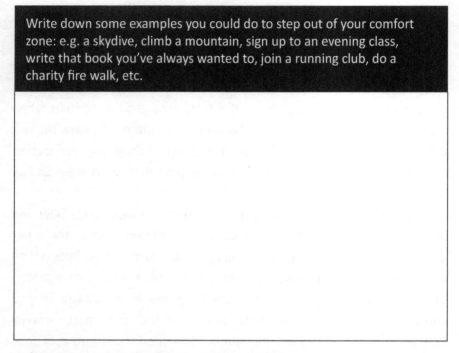

Write down some examples you could do to step out of your comfort zone: e.g. a skydive, climb a mountain, sign up to an evening class, write that book you've always wanted to, join a running club, do a charity fire walk, etc.

# Education, learning and knowledge

You can always learn more and gain more knowledge no matter who you are or how old you are. Education is important and there is an unlimited supply of information that can be beneficial for you in so many ways. Moreover, if by building your knowledge and learning more you can improve your health, both mentally and physically, and become happier, then it has to be worth making some effort.

Learn about the brain chemistry, the effects of food on mood, the benefits of exercise, the issues around stress, how medication works, tools and techniques to prevent depression, how to cope with difficult situations, how to increase confidence, how to be happier, etc.

Read books, use the Internet for research, find articles, speak to and listen to experts and you will become more educated and more knowledgeable. You are likely to feel you have more control, feel more confident, and be better placed to make the right choices for yourself and to advise others who may turn to you for help.

## Sense of perspective

We very often lose a sense of perspective, especially with all the stresses and hassles of modern life, but hopefully this little story about a mayonnaise jar will help.

*A professor stood before his philosophy class and had some items in front of him. When the class began, he wordlessly picked up a very large and empty mayonnaise jar and proceeded to fill it with golf balls. He then asked the students if the jar was full. They agreed that it was.*

*The professor then picked up a box of pebbles and poured them into the jar. He shook the jar lightly and the pebbles rolled into the open areas between the golf balls. He then asked the students again if the jar was full and they agreed it was. He next picked up a box of sand and poured it into the jar. Of course, the sand filled up everything else and he asked once more if the jar was full. The students responded with a unanimous "yes".*

*"Now," said the professor, "I want you to recognise that this jar represents your life. The golf balls are the important things – your family, your children, your health, your friends and your favourite passions – and if everything else was lost and only they remained, your life would still be full. The pebbles are the other things that matter, but if necessary you could cast off, like your job, your house and your car. The sand is everything else; the small stuff."*

*"If you put the sand into the jar first," he continued, "there is no room for the pebbles or the golf balls."*

"The same goes for life. If you spend all your time and energy on the small stuff, you will never have room for the things that are important to you. So first pay attention to the things that are critical to your happiness.

Spend quality time with your nearest and dearest, take time to get medical check-ups, take care of the golf balls first, the things that really matter, and set your priorities, as the rest is just sand."

## Eye exercise

It can be very easy to take on too much and feel like you are overwhelmed with everything, whether that is at work, domestically, or a combination of both – being pushed and pulled everywhere, deadlines to meet, a never-ending 'to-do' list, constant demands on your time, pressures to deliver, and basically feeling like there is no end to the stress.

If you imagine all the things that are going on in your life causing you this stress are large boxes that are lined up in front of you, across your vision, then you will notice that your vision is blocked and you cannot see beyond these boxes. You are in a position where all you see is these boxes, obstacles in front of you, and you can no longer see beyond this. Your long-term, bigger-picture view is blocked by all these short-term, stressful things that are taking over your life. Visualise this picture where all the boxes are lined up and all you can see is them blocking your view.

Now the next bit of advice is not some miracle cure to all the problems and stresses you face but it may help you see things a little more clearly and thus reduce the stress. Imagine once more all these boxes, but instead of them lined up across your vision, move them so they are lined up, one at a time, in front of you going backwards so you can only see the first box, although all the others are lined up behind. What you will now notice is that your vision is much clearer, as, although you can see the first box, you are able to see either side and beyond it, thus the bigger picture, the long-term view, is restored.

You are only human and you cannot do everything, so try to line up all the stresses, demands, pressure – and therefore the boxes – in such a way that your vision is not blocked. Prioritise what to focus on, one at a time, and those boxes will gradually reduce, which will mean you can keep a sense of perspective and your stress levels will fall.

## Focusing too much on certain things

Sometimes we can let certain objectives that we have spoil our lives and let them have a very negative effect on how we feel and behave. We may have plans, objectives, hopes, ambitions, targets, etc. in our lives that will generally be positive and beneficial, but we must be careful not to cross the line with these and make them damaging to our wellbeing.

For example, quite often people who are single focus so much on wanting to find a partner, believing that being single is not good and being in a relationship will make them feel happy. This constant thought that they need to find someone, and their view that there is something wrong with being single, will have a constant negative effect on them. They live every day unhappy because they are single, blaming any low feelings on this status, whereas it is far more likely that this thinking is the cause of any problems rather than the actual fact that they are not in a relationship.

It could be that someone is so desperate to get married, have children and therefore have their own family that all the time this is not happening they feel less happy, more down on themselves, becoming more anxious and focusing so much on what they don't have, what they think they want and what they think will make them happy, that they cannot enjoy their current life. They are causing the unhappiness by this thinking and focusing, whereas if they spent less time on this they would feel much happier and better about themselves.

There are many other examples where people impose unhappiness, even misery, upon themselves, by believing that something they don't have currently will make them happy, and until they get what they are after they remain unhappy and unfulfilled. There are many people who are always trying to achieve more wealth, believing that the more money they have, the happier they will be. They can spend so much time focused on generating wealth, making sacrifices, feeling unhappy and unsatisfied, and they may never get to the position they want. And if they do achieve the wealth they were after they realise that actually it doesn't make them happy and they have wasted so much of their time ignoring far more important things in their life.

## Excuses and barriers

We are so good at coming up with excuses or reasons we can't do something or why something has happened a certain way. Additionally, there are so often barriers stopping us achieving something that are actually false barriers we have put up ourselves. In fact, a lot of time and energy is spent on coming up with the excuses, and putting these false barriers in place, that do not help us and prevent us from doing so much more with our lives and improving the quality of that life.

How often have you found yourself saying or thinking that you cannot do something? There is a barrier in your way which is preventing you. For example, there is not enough time, a lack of money, nobody to go with, I won't be able to do it, takes too long, they won't understand, I don't know how to do it, or what if it doesn't work? In most cases these are self-imposed barriers that don't need to be there and you have the ability to remove these barriers or step over them. Be honest with yourself, and if they are false barriers then do not let them hold you back.

There can be genuine reasons that you are not able to do something but there is a difference between a reason and an excuse. If you find yourself coming up with excuses for not doing something, or for feeling or behaving in a certain way, then be honest with yourself and recognise that they are just excuses that are unproductive and will prevent you moving forward as you could.

| Examples of common reasons or barriers given by people why they can't do something | Is this an excuse or a false barrier? | Or is it a genuine reason? |
|---|---|---|
| I can't afford to eat healthily. It costs a lot more money to eat healthily and at the moment it is just too expensive. | | |
| I don't have time to take a break or go on holiday. I have so much to do with work that any time off will have to wait. | | |
| Nobody will understand how I feel so there is no point even asking for help. | | |
| I've got dodgy knees which always hurt if I exercise so I will just have to accept exercise is not for me. | | |
| I've got so many responsibilities and things I have to do for the kids and family and at work that I just don't have time to do my own things that I would like to do. | | |
| There are lots of things I would like to do but I have nobody to do them with. | | |
| Things always seem to go wrong so there's no point even trying anymore. | | |

'Excuses will always be there for you. Opportunity won't.'

## Social activities, not isolation

Humans are generally very social animals and it is natural for us to be around other people. Talking and communicating with each other, sharing and doing things together, having physical contact, being within social groups, and spending time with each other. We do this for many reasons and it is natural and also beneficial. If we stay away from people, or become reclusive or socially isolated, this is usually due to problems we have and negative issues we are experiencing.

A common symptom of depression is not wanting to socialise and becoming more reclusive. And this isolation usually makes things worse so it is important to try and maintain social activities as much as possible. There will, of course, be times when you need your own space and it will be too much for you to go out and be social and that is OK, but please make sure that it doesn't become a habit or you get used to being isolated.

If you are isolated, you start to lose social and communication skills, your confidence will most likely decrease, you will become used to being on your own and not interacting with others, you will spend more time thinking, which is likely to be more negative than positive, and you will lose friends and contacts if you don't stay in touch. Loneliness can be both a cause and an effect of depression, so there is a need to try and do something about it.

Write down a list of all the things you can do over the next few weeks which will get you meeting people, seeing people, talking to people, getting out of the house and being more

social. E.g. go out for a meal with family or friends, join a book club, take a visit to the shopping centre, meet a work colleague for a coffee, attend a talk at your local theatre, or go to a football or cricket match.

## Facebook and Twitter

In recent years, there has been an enormous change in how people communicate, and sites such as Facebook and Twitter have had a huge effect and influence. In many ways they are fantastic, entertaining, a great way of communicating, making friends, etc., with a wide range of benefits. However, there are also risks involved and there is often a fine balance between the beneficial aspects and things that can be harmful and unproductive, particularly if you are struggling with your own problems.

If you are feeling low, upset, angry, depressed, then it is all too easy to express that on these sites, often in a negative and unhelpful way. You may be crying out for help, letting out frustrations, seeking attention, hoping someone will understand or wanting someone to wave a magic wand for you. Sometimes it will be beneficial and you will receive some help and support as a result. However, reacting negatively, lashing out, writing without thinking, saying stuff you don't really mean, being very negative, moaning about everything and not being constructive in any way can cause more issues than they solve.

Generally, people don't like to hear negative stuff and often don't know how to react or know what to do for the best. The answers you are looking for, the help and support you want, are unlikely to be achieved by this method. Friends you have and people who care about you will be concerned, but will be unsure how to respond and quite often will not respond, making you feel like they don't care. Also, there is a lot of potential for misunderstandings and misinterpretations that can lead to further problems, as it is difficult to explain everything in a few words or sentences.

You can also find yourself becoming stuck behind a computer, laptop, or phone, and therefore isolated from real human contact and communication. It is important not to hide yourself away like this and avoid people, with only online communication.

Use Facebook and Twitter and other sites if it can be beneficial to you, but beware of the downsides, and particularly if you are struggling you may be better off using those methods of communicating less, or not at all, and instead focusing on more face-to-face or verbal contact.

## Men and women – differences

There is a well-known book called *Men Are from Mars, Women Are from Venus*. This book tries to explain that there are some fundamental differences between men and women, including the way they deal with problems. Although a generalisation, I believe that there is a lot of truth in the differences and by understanding these then a lot of upset, grief, pain, and anger can be avoided and difficult situations dealt with much better.

I will try to explain as best I can about the main differences and therefore what you should try to do to improve the situation with regard to personal relationships. If a man is faced with a problem, or is going through a difficult time, then he will typically want to sort this out by himself. He will be reluctant to ask for help and will not want to discuss or talk about the problem or issues. He will most likely go to his 'cave' where he will want to be left alone to sort out his own issues. He will not want to burden anyone else and will probably go quiet and distance himself from his wife/girlfriend.

His wife/girlfriend will realise something is up as she will notice him being quieter and more distant. Her instinct is to offer someone to talk to so she will go to his 'cave' and ask what the matter is. He will not want to be disturbed and does not want to burden anyone else, particularly his nearest and dearest, so he will remain quiet and say everything's fine. She will feel rejected and hurt as he continues to distance himself and she won't know what is wrong. However, once the man has come up with the answer, or rather what he thinks is the answer, to his problems, then he will leave the 'cave' and be much more upbeat, positive, and with a sense of achievement. Clearly, this is a big change in behaviour and mood and is difficult for the wife/girlfriend to understand, particularly as she has not been allowed to be involved, so she naturally feels a bit put out and finds it hard to share in her partner's newfound positivity.

On the other hand, if a woman has problems to deal with or is struggling to cope with things, then she will most likely want to talk about and share the information on the issues. She does not really want answers or a quick fix; she wants her partner to understand and share the problem by talking. The man's instinct is to try and find a solution and give her the answer to the problem as quickly as possible. So very often he will interrupt her and tell her his solution, believing that he is helping and doing the right thing. She will see this very differently as her interpretation is that he has not been listening, he doesn't understand, he doesn't care, and he is interrupting her while she is trying to talk with him. She will feel upset and annoyed and her reaction will show, which will then confuse the man, who is expecting praise for giving her some answers to the problems.

Very quickly and easily and through neither party's fault you can see how often arguments can develop with upset, anger, and frustration occurring, and often the situation is made much worse than the original issues at hand. So the best advice for a woman is to just give her partner space and let him be in his 'cave' undisturbed until he is ready to come out, and when he does, then try to share his renewed enthusiasm. And for a man that he must never try to interrupt and offer answers to his partner; instead he should just listen and agree and empathise as much as possible.

A lot of upset, stress, and pain can be avoided if both partners understand the differences and can then empathise and act accordingly.

# Reflect and step back

Behaviours and thoughts, such as being reactive, jealousy, making comparisons, making assumptions and judgements, negative thinking and looking to blame someone, or something, will very rarely be beneficial at all. Yet, they are common behaviours and thoughts, especially when feeling low. In order to feel better and overcome the issues facing you, then one of the best things you should try to focus on is reflection.

Taking a few steps back and reflecting on the situation and circumstances, or indeed stopping and reflecting on your life, will allow you to consider many more factors. It will also allow you to gain a better sense of perspective, give you time to think and then say what you really believe.

It can be difficult to take a step back, especially when you have a wave of negative emotion that could be frustration, stress, or anger, so it is important to first recognise this emotion building and then act to ensure as much as possible you reflect first, rather than react first. Initially it could be techniques such as counting to ten, doing a few very deep breaths, singing a favourite song, pacing up and down for a short while – basically anything that will allow you to step back for a moment.

Then you are in a better position to be able to do some reflection. Take more time to think, consider the situation in a more pragmatic way, understand the issues, gain some real perspective, make sure all factors have been taken into account and then decide what the next steps will be, if there are any.

'Too many people overvalue what they are not and don't have, and undervalue what they are and do have.'

**CHAPTER 6 SUMMARY**

This chapter has been quite long, looking at even more factors that potentially affect your depression and can be understood so you can beat it. I hope you have taken your time with each and really thought carefully about how they impact on you and your life. As I have said all along, there is no one answer or instant miracle cure; however, by looking at all the possible factors and influences you can work out what has most impact and what areas you can work on that will be best for you. Remember to go back and reread at anytime. Your understanding is building, your control is growing, and combined with the new tools and techniques you have developed, you are getting stronger each day and there will only be one winner in this fight against depression.

# Chapter 7
# Dealing With The Bad Days

*Objectives:*
*This chapter is all about your defences, your resilience, and your ability*
*to deal with and manage any problems. It is often said that it is less*
*important what happens to you, and much more important how you*
*handle it and react to it. So let's build up those defences, become more*
*resilient, and feel confident in our ability to deal with anything that life*
*has to throw at us going forward.*

## YOUR DEFENCES AND DEALING WITH THE BAD DAYS

### Bad days are inevitable and normal

Everyone, no matter who you are, will experience bad days in his or her life, and sometimes for no obvious reasons. Often the bad days are a direct result of certain events, circumstances, experiences, or people doing or saying something you don't like. There is also the possibility of misunderstandings, an overreaction, or even the expectation that you will have a bad day actually creating a bad day due to the negative thinking.

Some bad days are inevitable and normal, and you cannot go through life without some bad days. However, firstly you need to ensure that you minimise these bad days as much as you can, and then when they do happen you deal with them effectively. So, in addition to all the previous chapters here are some key areas to ensure you do have strong defences and can deal with those bad days.

# Do not feel sorry for yourself

Particularly when you are depressed and you have a bad day it is very easy to feel sorry for yourself. I have already mentioned how unproductive and helpful this is in general, but particularly as you are beating the depression and doing the right things it becomes a huge temptation to go back to feeling sorry for yourself on an inevitable bad day that comes along. Do not do it!

It will not help you and it is a bad habit, a bad OLD habit that you will no longer do. Instead of feeling sorry for yourself you will go and do something productive and positive to deal with the bad day. Go to your toolbox and choose something. Your defences will become much stronger if you do not feel sorry for yourself. Each time you are given a reason where many people would go down that negative and unproductive route of self-pity, you will make sure you don't. And each time you don't, you become stronger and your defences become more solid.

# Get the facts

It is so important wherever possible to get the facts with regard to anything that affects you and may cause a bad day. You hear some bad news, someone says something you don't like, that letter or email doesn't arrive, you don't get a reply to a text you sent, or you start to feel unwell. So many examples of things that can happen to you, where you jump to conclusions and make assumptions in a negative way which has an effect on your mood and how you are dealing with your depression.

In many of these cases you will not have all the facts and the reality is different from what you presume. Your presumptions can set you back and cause additional issues. However, if you make sure, as much as you can, that you have all the facts first then you will be in a much stronger position because you will wait for the facts and the reality. And the reality is likely, quite often, to not be as bad.

So as a way of dealing with bad days and building your defences make sure you always wait or look to get all the facts before you react or think the worst. Get into that habit and you will be much stronger and more resilient.

## Bad things happen every day

Unfortunately, no matter who you are or what your situation is, there will be bad things that happen every day to millions of people all over the world. It is called life and whether you think so or not you will not be alone in having bad days or bad experiences or bad luck. Especially when you are feeling low and something goes wrong, you will naturally feel more unlucky, picked upon, or have the feeling that nothing will ever go right. However, it is not just you, and bad things do happen. You have to accept that and understand that things will go wrong or you will have some bad luck. Many things that create a bad day are out of your control and it just happens; that is life. Life is not fair in that way. If you realise and accept this, then whenever something does go wrong you won't take it so personally or to heart. It won't cause such stress and turmoil or send your mood spiralling lower.

Instead, you will take it for what it is, similarly to millions of other people each day. You can choose to let it cause big issues or to accept it happens, and you will deal with it in the best way possible and appreciate it could have been a lot worse. Your defences will be stronger as a result going forward.

## Mistakes and misunderstandings happen

There will be times when you will make a mistake or misunderstand something and so will everybody else. Nobody is perfect and for many reasons these mistakes and misunderstandings can happen that may cause some issues to you. It could be that you get angry, annoyed, and upset with yourself as a result, or you may have those feelings related to someone else.

If you allow it, then these inevitable but unintentional mistakes and misunderstandings could cause you further problems. Your anger could build, your mood could dip lower, you may do or say something you regret and your defences could be weakened because of the way you handle the situation. So instead remember that mistakes and misunderstandings happen all the time and are usually unintentional. Don't be so hard on yourself or other people who are responsible, and recognise that these things will always happen, and if you can react in a pragmatic, rational, and empathetic way then it will be much better for you and you can remain strong with your defences intact.

## Negative expectations

For most people, when suffering with depression, they will often have negative thoughts that relate to the past, the present, and the future. Their expectations will be more negative and therefore they will live their life anticipating negative things happening to them. Unfortunately this is common and can have a big impact on how quickly someone beats depression and how strong their defences are in managing it going forward.

If you expect a negative life, then you are more likely to obtain that. You will be more susceptible to negative experiences and thoughts, and you will be weaker as a result. So the less negative your expectations, the better, and indeed the more positive your expectations, then that will be better still.

Your defences will be stronger and you will deal better with future events and situations if your expectations are more positive. That is a mindset, and something you can control. It may not be easy and will require effort and practice, but you will be in a much better position if you focus on positive thinking and expectations rather than having the unhelpful and damaging negative expectations.

## Everything is temporary

It is worth knowing that pretty much everything in life is temporary, and that includes both the good things and the bad things. Having that knowledge can be very beneficial. With regard to the good stuff you are more likely to embrace it, to enjoy it more, to value it and to not take it for granted. Moreover, when it comes to the bad stuff you know that it won't last.

When you are going through depression, having bad days, when things are going against you, when life isn't fair and you are in despair, remember it is only temporary. Things will change, good stuff will happen, you will receive some good news and get that break you want – it is inevitable. You don't know what the future holds or what is around the corner so just because you are having a bad day, bad week, or bad month it doesn't mean that good stuff won't happen soon.

There are so many people I know and whom I have talked to when they have been in despair, feeling like there is no hope, and can't see how anything good will happen to them. Yet, in all cases, down the line things have changed and good things have happened. Perhaps that has been several months later but it has happened and they always say that for anyone going through similar to what they were, then they have to remember that the pain, anguish, and despair are only temporary.

Use that knowledge to be patient, have belief, and to be more resilient to the challenges life throws at you.

'Everything in life is temporary. So if things are going good, enjoy it and if things are going bad, don't worry; it can't last forever.'

## Rocky quote and boxing analogy

Many of you would have heard of the actor Sylvester Stallone and the *Rocky* films he wrote, directed, and starred in about a boxer who triumphed over adversity. In the sixth and final film of the series, called *Rocky Balboa*, there is a scene where the boxer is talking to his grown-up son during an argument and I believe there are several very poignant and important messages he gets across. This has become one of my favourite quotes, or rather, series of quotes. Here it is:

*"Then the time came for you to be your own man and take on the world, and you did. But somewhere along the line, you changed. You stopped being you. You let people stick a finger in your face and tell you you're no good. And when things got hard, you started looking for something to blame, like a big shadow. Let me tell you something you already know. The world ain't all sunshine and rainbows. It's a very mean and nasty place and I don't care how tough you are, it will beat you to your knees and keep you there permanently if you let it. You, me, or nobody is going to hit as hard as life. But it ain't about how hard you hit. It's about how hard you can get hit and keep moving forward. How much you can take and keep moving forward. That's how winning is done! Now if you know what you're worth then go out and get what you're worth. But you've got to be willing to take the hits, and not pointing fingers saying you ain't where you want to be because of him, or her, or anybody! Cowards do that and that ain't you! You're better than that! I'm always going*

*to love you no matter what. No matter what happens. You're my son and you're my blood. You're the best thing in my life. But until you start believing in yourself, you ain't going to have a life."*

There are several good points and things to consider above, but one of the key ones is about the fact that it's not about how hard you hit but how you deal with getting hit. You need good defences and all the best boxers will focus more on their defence than their attack. Being able to avoid the hits, block the hits, and if necessary absorb the hits is key to victory. And in life you will succeed if you have strong defences.

If you can develop your defences it will give you great strength, courage, and confidence because you will start to realise that no matter what life throws at you and no matter how hard it hits, you can take it. You can avoid, block, or absorb those hits. You can take whatever comes your way. You will realise that although at times it's uncomfortable and you would  rather not be receiving those hits, they do not hurt you or weaken you, and they actually make you stronger.

Visualise being in a boxing ring, and life is throwing all these punches at you, yet you can take it and you know that your defences are stronger than anything that life can hit you with. What a great feeling knowing you can deal with it and you won't lose and also the fact your time will come when you can start throwing some hits back and ultimately you are going to succeed and come out victorious.

## Sense of humour

It is very easy whilst going through depression to lose our sense of humour, and understandably so. When you feel low and are thinking negatively it is hard to laugh and joke and see the funny side of things. However, it is really important to laugh, joke, have some fun, watch comedy, have some banter, and smile! We want to enjoy our lives more and be happier and we are all capable of laughter and we can enjoy laughing, even if we may not feel in a particularly jolly, laughter-inducing mood.

It is often in those times when we need to make the effort to find our sense of humour.

There are so many things that can, and do, make us laugh, so seek those out. It could be a comedy programme, a funny film, some jokes you find on the Internet, watching funny clips on YouTube, meeting up with friends for some banter and telling stories, doing some silly dancing, or pulling funny faces in front of the mirror. There are so many things that you can do to bring some laughter to your life, and the benefits from improving your mood are worth that effort, and a sense of humour is a great way to build up your defences to fight depression.

Plus it is vital that you can still laugh at yourself, too. Allow yourself to laugh. Don't feel guilty about having some fun, smiling, and laughing when you are supposed to be depressed. You can have depression, or can be beating depression, and still be capable of laughing and joking. So the next time you have a bad day try using humour as your defence in dealing with it and beating the depression.

'Let your smile change the world. Don't let the world change your smile.'

## Learn to dance in the rain

There are many uncertainties in life but there are also many certainties, like the fact that life will always throw up challenges for us to deal with. Also, everyone is different, with different circumstances, abilities, skills, and opportunities, but again that is life. You may be disadvantaged in some way, you may have some bad luck, things may go against you and life may seem unfair. But a great quote that recognises this and also recognises that it is your life and you only get one shot at it is: *"you don't have to wait for the storm to pass if you learn to dance in the rain".*

Try to make the most of your circumstances, your skills, your situation, and your abilities. Nothing is perfect and the rain will fall at times, so get out there and dance in that rain. If every day was warm and sunny with blue skies then you would soon stop appreciating it and life would become quite boring. Embrace and appreciate those sunny days and make the most of them, but don't let the dark days stop you living your life. Learn to deal with the challenges and the inevitable difficulties that arise in life and that way your life will be a whole lot better and more rewarding for you and others.

## You will be so much stronger from this experience

In some ways having depression is a blessing, because once you beat it you have so much more strength and power knowing that nothing ever again can be so bad – and if you can beat depression you can succeed at anything.

You might not recognise this now, but in the future it is likely that you will reflect on your depression and come to the conclusion that you are a stronger and better person as a result of your experiences. You no longer have to fear anything as you know you can deal with whatever comes your way. You know you will never ever be as low as you once were and you came through that anyway. You will be better placed to help others and make a real difference to other people's lives.

The actor Michael J Fox (the *Back to the Future* guy!) was diagnosed with Parkinson's disease in his early thirties, at the height of his success in the film and TV industry, yet he called his autobiography *Lucky Man*. This was because on reflection he believed that getting the disease when he did was a huge blessing and made his life so much better. Now that sounds crazy on the face of it, yet his explanation was that for many years prior to his illness he was an arrogant, rude, selfish alcoholic who treated people really badly and was basically not a nice person. The diagnosis was a massive wake-up call and changed his life completely to one where he stopped drinking, treated people with respect, gained humility, focused on helping others, and became a much better person. He saw himself as being lucky to have been able to change his life around as a result of the Parkinson's disease.

In a similar way it is possible that in the future you will consider yourself lucky to have had the experience of depression. Remember that!

Please use the table below to think about, and then write down, examples of things that may happen to cause a bad day or that would get you down and make your depression worse. Write down how you would have previously reacted to this typically, and then write how you will now be dealing with the same situation.

| An example of a bad day? | What you may previously have done? | What you will now do instead? |
|---|---|---|
| e.g. you get a car tyre puncture on your way to work. It is raining so you get wet, you are late for Work, and it costs you £100 to get a new tyre. | Got very angry and upset and felt sorry for myself which would have lasted all day. Believed it was another example of my bad luck. | Accept that it was unfortunate but these things happen to people every day. Laugh at the fact that it just happened to be raining and realising that it could have been much worse and the hassle, and £100 is not the end of the world and it has to be put into perspective. Go to the toolbox and do something positive and productive. |
|  |  |  |
|  |  |  |

## CHAPTER 7 SUMMARY

This chapter has been focused on building your defences and coping better with the bad days that will always come about, no matter who you are. Life will always throw some curve balls at you, but it is about how you deal with those and how you respond. Going through depression will make you stronger and, although it is a horrible thing to have to go through, you will soon become invincible knowing that you have beaten depression and you have the tools, techniques, knowledge, and resilience to never let depression affect you again.

You are stronger than you think and you will only get even stronger – so keep going, the final chapter is nearly here.

# Chapter 8

# You Now Control Your Ship

*Objectives:*
*Your final chapter of the book is all about recapping what you have learned and understood, using the tools and techniques you have acquired, utilising your toolbox, practising and using the knowledge you now have, and realising you are now in control of your ship!*

## Keep learning and doing the right things

The main thing I have learned about depression from my own experiences, lots of research, and speaking to many others is that although it is very beatable you have to keep learning and doing the right things in order to prevent it returning. Far too many people who manage to overcome depression then fail to manage themselves and depression comes back. It is unfortunate but it is also a reality that people stop doing the things that work and default back to old habits, become complacent, and the depression returns. Make sure that does not happen to you. It is likely that you are more susceptible or predisposed to depression than many other people, and so it is essential that you recognise any signals, triggers, or circumstances that may affect you and ensure you do all those things that you know will work. Use those tools and techniques. If you keep practising, seek to understand yourself even more and do the right things, then you will always be able to prevent depression coming back. I am

100% confident that I will never suffer with depression again due to my improved knowledge and understanding, combined with being skilled in the use of those tools and techniques that work for me. You can be the same.

## Keep using your toolbox

I hope you have been using your toolbox! It really is a very powerful thing if used well. You should never be in a position where you cannot do something to improve the situation. Whenever you need to, you can go to your toolbox and take something out to use there and then to help.

The spiral of decline should become a thing of the past because now, and going forward, as soon as you recognise a downward shift in your mood, thoughts, feelings, and behaviour you can push it back up again by using your toolbox. What a powerful thing it is to have that control where you can use your tools in any situation to improve things, and the more you practise and the wider range of tools you have, the better and easier it will be. Keep adding new things to your toolbox, trying stuff out, replacing things if they need replacing or upgrading to better tools! What works for some people won't work for others and on some days there will be tools that aren't that effective for whatever reason, but on other days they are ideal. It is also helpful to keep your toolbox organised so you know what you have and where they are so you can easily find them whenever you need to.

## YOU CONTROL THE SHIP NOW

## Internal vs. external

Remember how important it is to be more internal in your thinking and behaviour so that you have a greater sense of power, control, and influence over your life. This will increase your confidence, provide more certainty, and empower you more. It is your life, where you are the one most responsible for what you do and how you do it.

The more external you think, then the more disempowering this is and the greater uncertainty there will be for you. Your life shouldn't be controlled by luck, fate, other people, superstition, horoscopes, Tarot cards, or wishful thinking. You should control your life as much as possible, and you can be in control. Believe in yourself, take responsibility, be who you are and be the captain of your own ship.

## Understand who you are

We are all different, with varying genetics, upbringings, environments, and experiences that shape our thinking and behaviour. We react differently to event with some things affecting others in a wide range of ways with sometimes no obvious reason. The fact is we are all unique and no one solution fits all. Therefore, it is vital that, as much as possible, we understand ourselves and who we are. Why do we react, respond, feel, think, act, and behave the way we do. Why do certain things affect us the way they do and what can we do that will work for us. By understanding ourselves, we have a much greater chance of being in control and overcoming any issues we have or will face going forward. So take the time and make the effort to really understand who you are – it will be worth it.

## Your brain

Everything you do, think, say, and feel, and how you behave are as a result of what your brain tells you. Millions of messages each day are sent inside your brain and understanding more about your brain and how it works will be very helpful to you. It is the most amazing and complex organ, but the more we understand it, the better placed we are to make the best use of it.

Having knowledge about the brain chemicals and neurotransmitters will help you make sense of some of the highs and lows you feel. Having the understanding related to the Chimp Paradox will help you make sense of your behaviour and why you do and say what you do.

# Recognise any triggers

From understanding yourself better and working out how certain things will cause a negative reaction to our wellbeing we can then do something to help ourselves. That could be to avoid the situation, person, or event. It could be to see how we can change the situation so it doesn't cause an issue, it could be to learn to try and minimise the effect it has on us, or it could be to learn how to cope better and deal with the situation or experience.

If you are aware of these 'triggers' that may cause problems then you must recognise them and put into action some kind of response that will be beneficial to you or limit any damage. Do not just let it happen or blindly ignore the triggers. Being both self-aware and aware of the triggers will allow you to be more in control and make better choices as to what you then do.

# Use your toolbox

Using your toolbox is the most effective and simple day-to-day method of overcoming and managing your depression. You never ever have to think or say again that there is nothing you can do to help yourself. Whenever you start to feel down, or find yourself with the dark clouds rolling in, then it should become an automatic, instinctive response to now go to your toolbox and find something that will help at that given time.

It could be as simple as playing some music or reading a quote, talking to a friend or cooking a meal. Your toolbox should have so many options that there will always be something for you to use. How powerful is that – to know that you can always do something to help yourself, to be in control and lift yourself back up again?

## Positive vs. negative

For a long time you have probably had more negativity than positivity in your life. You can change that. You know the difference between what is negative and what is positive, and if you focus and keep practising being positive your whole mindset will become much more positive.

Negative thinking will not help in any way. It will only compound the problems you have. You have a choice and you can choose to do, to think, to say, to feel, to behave in a positive way. Of course it will be hard at times, and you won't feel like it, but you still have a choice. Choose to be positive and it will bring positive changes to your life.

## Productive vs. unproductive

In a similar way to the positive vs. negative above, it is likely that you have spent a long time doing too many unproductive things ,rather than productive ones. Again you know the difference between the two and you have the choice as to which you take.

As much as possible do things that are productive and whenever you do, acknowledge it and give yourself a pat on the back. It's not easy to be productive when you are going through depression, but it can be done and the more you do, the easier it becomes and the greater the results. Being unproductive is not just unhelpful, it is likely to make things worse and you definitely don't want that. So keep asking yourself, "is this productive or unproductive?" Or "do I want to feel better or not?" as they are basically the same thing.

## Your defences and coping skills

You are stronger than you think and you can deal with more than you realise. You can also become even stronger and will eventually realise you can deal with anything and cope with anything. With the right tools, techniques, knowledge, and defences you are invincible. Yes, you will still have bad days and low points but going forward you will know that nothing can beat you – certainly not depression.

Don't become complacent: keep working on those defences. The more you do, the more powerful and in control you become. Your confidence and self-belief will continue to increase and depression will become a thing of the past.

## Keep doing the right things

It goes without saying that if you stop doing the things that work, then the likelihood is that things will get worse again. You must keep doing the right things. You can always learn, always improve and always become even stronger.

You now have so many tools and techniques to use, so much more knowledge and understanding and so much more power and control over your life. Keep practising and it will only get better. You've done most of the hard work and now it is time to reap the benefits, do more things you enjoy and want to do, and look forward to your life ahead.

## Stay in control – it's your ship

It is your life and it is your ship: you are the captain. You are in control of your ship and you can decide where you want to go. Keep an eye on the compass, the control panel, the satellites, etc, but also enjoy the views along your journey.

You can't do much about the weather, but if a storm does come along you now know your ship can handle it and you can do what is needed to sail through any choppy waters and you will soon have the peaceful, calm waters and blue sky with sunshine again.

### CHAPTER 8 SUMMARY

So the final chapter is over and it was primarily focused on recapping the many important areas that you need to understand, consider, think about, and apply. There has been a lot of information to digest and think about, so make sure you go back over any areas you want to, or feel you need to.

This is your book and it is your life – so make the most of it.

For many people who get through depression by doing the right things, it is not the end of depression; as they stop doing the right things, the depression comes back. Make sure you are not one of those people – you can beat depression for good! You have the knowledge, understanding, control, tools, and techniques. Depression never has to affect you again, and you are also so much stronger now having gone through it – remember that.

# Here is a table highlighting some of my personal thoughts from my experience with depression:

| What I did well during my depression | What I did badly during my depression | What I wish I had done during my depression |
| --- | --- | --- |
| – I was pretty good at exercising and being active by making myself go running and still going to the gym fairly regularly<br><br>– I set myself a few physical challenges, including a couple of marathons, which gave me a positive focus and then a real sense of achievement and pride<br><br>– I rarely allowed myself to feel sorry for myself and if I did it was only for a short period of time<br><br>– I took responsibility for my situation and looked to find answers myself<br><br>– I never turned to alcohol or drugs<br><br>– After the initial period I was good at looking at the future, believing things would get better and planning things to look forward to | – I was very critical and hard on myself and blamed myself for the situation<br><br>– I hardly spoke to anyone about my situation and how I was feeling – I never asked for help and thought nobody could possibly understand or help me<br><br>– I focused far too much on the money and sacrificed so much of my life due to that<br><br>– I would let the smallest thing, setback, or bad news make me angry and upset, so my sense of perspective was not good<br><br>– I distanced myself and stopped seeing friends and that meant I lost contact and friendships as a result | – I wish I had talked more to friends or others to explain my situation<br><br>– I wish I had stayed in touch with more friends and been more social and not shut myself away<br><br>– I wish I had read more books on depression and done more research as that would have meant I would have beaten it much sooner<br><br>– I wish I had been nicer to myself, given myself a break and a few treats from time to time<br><br>– I wish I had discovered and used my toolbox much earlier<br><br>– I wish I had allowed myself to laugh more and do some of the things I enjoyed |

| | | |
|---|---|---|
| – I was good at just going for a walk with some music to get out of the house and reflect and clear my mind<br><br>– I was good at searching and finding inspiring stories to keep me motivated and to pick me up when feeling really low | – To an extent I lost my sense of humour. I felt that I couldn't laugh, smile or be happy because I should be miserable<br><br>– I got used to being sad, miserable and unhappy and almost accepted that was how it was | – I wish I had found a mentor or someone who could advise and give me some better direction at the time |

# Final thoughts

I really hope this book has been beneficial to you . I know how hard it can be both going through depression and trying to beat it. Please keep using this book and reread whenever you need to, as often some of the things mentioned need to be read more than once. This is your book to look at and refer to whenever you want.

I would love to hear from you with any comments or feedback, and hopefully hear how the book has helped you. Please feel free to contact me via email: info@climbyourmountain.org.

Best wishes

Charlie Wardle
Founder of Climb Your Mountain (CYM)

# More from the Charity

Climb Your Mountain (CYM) was set up as a charity in 2008 with the aim of helping anyone who is going through a difficult time in their life by helping them to climb their own personal mountain. It is for anybody, any age, and any background, and recognises that stress, depression, low confidence, health issues, associated conditions and lack of general wellbeing can be damaging and can affect anybody for many different reasons.

The charity has two main focuses. Firstly, there is an emphasis on using physical exercise and activities as a way of dealing with, managing, preventing and treating issues. There is a wide range of benefits to physical exercise and activities, yet it is often hard to motivate yourself, especially when you are feeling low. Also, many people are not aware of the huge benefits that physical exercise and activities can have on your mental health and wellbeing, as well as your physical health.

So the charity provides opportunities as well as encouragement and motivation for people to do more exercise and take part in more physical activities. We have organised hundreds of free walks, hikes, runs, climbs and cycle rides across the country, in a friendly and safe environment. Anyone can participate and people are there to benefit from enjoying the activities, meeting new people, seeing new places and becoming healthier and happier.

The second focus is on education and providing information and knowledge for people about physical and mental health and overall wellbeing. CYM offers free educational talks, courses and workshops that cover a wide range of topics including stress and depression (symptoms, causes, prevention, management and treatment), anxiety, brain chemistry, food and mood, benefits of exercise, confidence and self-esteem, motivation and barriers to wellbeing. There are also the self-help books that expand on the course content and can reach more people, offering practical help and advice, so they are in a better position to help themselves and to be able to help others.

Please visit the website www.climbyourmountain.org for more information and to get in touch. If you know of any groups, organisations or companies that would be interested in a talk or course, then get in touch.

## How you can help others

We rely heavily on donations and sponsorship to fund our services, including providing these free books. If you can help us in any way or would like to volunteer or be involved then you can help many other people. Please get in touch!

We also organise overseas treks and challenges as fundraising events for the charity with trips such as Kilimanjaro, Everest Base Camp trek, Pyrenees Thousand Lakes trek, Mount Toubkal, Great Wall of China trek, the Inca Trail, and others. So again, if interested get in touch!

Please email info@climbyourmountain.org

Or go to the website www.climbyourmountain.org

# Outdoor adventures & challenges

My main business away from the charity is organising outdoor trips, adventures and challenges, and you may be interested to see what is on offer. The website is www.themountaincoach.com.

There is a wide range of UK trips, challenges and adventures for all levels, including open events for the public and private groups. A great way to enjoy the outdoors, see new places, keep fit and healthy, boost your confidence, meet new people, make new friends, and generally have a great time!

# Company talks, workshops & seminars on

# Health & Wellbeing

In addition, I can deliver talks, workshops and seminars on a wide range of 'Health & Wellbeing' topics to groups, organisations and companies through the Climb Your Mountain charity.

If interested, please get in touch via:

Email: info@climbyourmountain.org
Website: www.climbyourmountain.org